European Political, Economic, and Security Issues

European Response to the Financial Crisis

EUROPEAN POLITICAL, ECONOMIC AND SECURITY ISSUES

The Land and Maritime Boundary Disputes of Europe
Rongxing Guo
2009. ISBN: 978-1-60741-628-9

Titanic 2010? The European Union and its Failed Lisbon Strategy
Arno Tausch (Editor)
2009. ISBN: 978-1-60741-826 -9

Faith and Reason of State: Lessons from Early Modern Europe and Cardinal Richelieu
AristotleTziampiris
2009. ISBN: 978-1-60741-949-5

Innovative Regulatory Approaches Coping with Scandinavian and European Union Policies
Noralv Veggeland (Editor)
2010. ISBN: 978-1-60876-673-4

European Response to the Financial Crisis
Baron L. Whitley (Editor)
2010. ISBN: 978-1-60876-817-2

EUROPEAN POLITICAL, ECONOMIC, AND SECURITY ISSUES

EUROPEAN RESPONSE TO THE FINANCIAL CRISIS

BARON L. WHITLEY
EDITOR

Nova Science Publishers, Inc.
New York

Copyright © 2010 by Nova Science Publishers, Inc.

All rights reserved. No part of this book may be reproduced, stored in a retrieval system or transmitted in any form or by any means: electronic, electrostatic, magnetic, tape, mechanical photocopying, recording or otherwise without the written permission of the Publisher.

For permission to use material from this book please contact us:
Telephone 631-231-7269; Fax 631-231-8175
Web Site: http://www.novapublishers.com

NOTICE TO THE READER

The Publisher has taken reasonable care in the preparation of this book, but makes no expressed or implied warranty of any kind and assumes no responsibility for any errors or omissions. No liability is assumed for incidental or consequential damages in connection with or arising out of information contained in this book. The Publisher shall not be liable for any special, consequential, or exemplary damages resulting, in whole or in part, from the readers' use of, or reliance upon, this material. Any parts of this book based on government reports are so indicated and copyright is claimed for those parts to the extent applicable to compilations of such works.

Independent verification should be sought for any data, advice or recommendations contained in this book. In addition, no responsibility is assumed by the publisher for any injury and/or damage to persons or property arising from any methods, products, instructions, ideas or otherwise contained in this publication.

This publication is designed to provide accurate and authoritative information with regard to the subject matter covered herein. It is sold with the clear understanding that the Publisher is not engaged in rendering legal or any other professional services. If legal or any other expert assistance is required, the services of a competent person should be sought. FROM A DECLARATION OF PARTICIPANTS JOINTLY ADOPTED BY A COMMITTEE OF THE AMERICAN BAR ASSOCIATION AND A COMMITTEE OF PUBLISHERS.

LIBRARY OF CONGRESS CATALOGING-IN-PUBLICATION DATA

European response to the financial crisis / editor, Baron L. Whitley.
   p. cm.
 Includes index.
 ISBN 978-1-60876-817-2 (softcover)
1. Financial crises--European Union countries. 2. Financial crises--Government policy--European Union countries. 3. European Union countries--Economic policy. I. Whitley, Baron L.
  HB3722.E97 2009 330.94--dc22
                                                         2009046472

Published by Nova Science Publishers, Inc. ✣ *New York*

CONTENTS

Preface vii

Chapter 1 Communication from the Commission to the European Council: A European Economic Recovery Plan 1
Commission of the European Communities

Chapter 2 The Financial Crisis: Impact on and Response by the European Union 25
James K. Jackson

Chapter 3 The U.S. Financial Crisis: Lessons from Sweden 75
James K. Jackson

Chapter 4 Iceland's Financial Crisis 83
James K. Jackson

Chapter 5 The U.S. Financial Crisis: The Response by Switzerland 93
James K. Jackson

Index 109

PREFACE

Some members of the European Union (EU) initially viewed the financial crisis as a purely American phenomenon. That view has changed as economic activity in the EU has declined at a fast pace over a short period of time. The authors of this book discuss the European Economic Recovery Plan, designed to exploit synergies and avoid negative spill-over effects through co-ordinated action, draw on all available policy levels, fiscal policies, structural and financial market reforms and external action and ensure full coherence between immediate actions and the EU's medium- to longer term objectives. This book provides an overview of the Swedish banking crisis and an explanation of the measures Sweden used to restore its banking system to health. Moreover, the recent experiences of Switzerland and other European countries (including Iceland, the UK, Sweden and Austria) raise questions about how national governments can effectively supervise large financial firms that operate across national borders. This book focuses on the development of organizational structures within national economies that can provide oversight of the different segments of the highly financial system. This book consists of public documents which have been located, gathered, combined, reformatted, and enhanced with a subject index, selectively edited and bound to provide easy access.

Chapter 1 - The global financial crisis has hit the EU hard. A squeeze on credit, falls in house prices and tumbling stock markets are all reinforcing a slump in consumer confidence, consumption and investment. Households are under real pressure. Businesses' order books are down. Sectors dependent on consumer credit – like private construction and the automobile industry – have seen their markets sharply deteriorate in many Member States.

The latest economic forecasts painted a bleak picture of close to zero growth and risks of contraction for the EU economy in 2009, with unemployment rising by some 2.7 million in the next two years, on the assumption that no corrective action is taken. In the weeks since the forecasts came out, economic conditions have deteriorated further.

Chapter 2 - According to the most recent National Threat Assessment, the global financial crisis and its geopolitical implications pose the primary near-term security concern of the United States. Over the short run, both the EU and the United States are attempting to resolve the financial crisis while stimulating domestic demand to stem the economic downturn. These efforts have born little progress so far as the economic recession and the financial crisis have become reinforcing events, causing EU governments to forge policy responses to both crises. In addition, both the United States and the EU likely will confront the prospect of growing economic and political instability in Eastern Europe and elsewhere over the impact of the economic recession on restive populations. In the long run, the United States and the EU likely will search for a regulatory scheme that provides for greater stability while not inadvertently offering advantages to any one country or group. Throughout the crisis, the European Central Bank and other central banks have assumed a critical role as the primary institutions with the necessary political and economic clout to respond effectively. Within Europe, national governments, private firms, and international organizations have varied in their response to the financial crisis, reflecting differing views over the proper policy course to pursue and the unequal effects of the financial crisis and the economic downturn. Initially, some EU members preferred to address the crisis on a case-by-case basis. As the crisis has persisted, however, leaders have begun looking for a systemic approach that ultimately may affect the drive within Europe toward greater economic integration.

Chapter 3 - In the early 1990s, Sweden faced a banking and exchange rate crisis that led it to rescue banks that had experienced large losses on their balance sheets and that threatened a collapse of the banking system. Some analysts and others argue that Sweden's experience could provide useful lessons for the execution and implementation of the Emergency Economic Stabilization Act of 2008[1]. The banking crisis facing the United States is unique, so there are no exact parallels from which to draw templates. Sweden's experience, however, represents a case study in how a systemic banking crisis was resolved in a developed country with democratic institutions. The Swedish central bank separated out good assets, which it left to the banks to oversee from bad assets, which it placed in a separate agency with broad authority to work out debt problems or to liquidate assets. Four lessons that emerged form Sweden's experience are: 1) the process must be transparent; 2) the resolution agency must be politically and financially independent; 3) market discipline must be maintained; and 4) there must be a plan to jump-start credit flows in the financial system. This report provides an overview of the Swedish banking crisis and an explanation of the measures Sweden used to restore its banking system to health.

Chapter 4 - On November 19, 2008, Iceland and the International Monetary Fund (IMF) finalized an agreement on a $6 billion economic stabilization program supported by a $2.1 billion loan from the IMF. Following the IMF decision, Denmark, Finland, Norway, and Sweden agreed to provide an additional $2.5 billion. Iceland's banking system had collapsed as a culmination of a series of decisions the banks made that left them highly exposed to disruptions in financial markets. The collapse of the banks also raises questions for U.S. leaders and others about supervising banks that operate across national borders, especially as it becomes increasingly difficult to distinguish the limits of domestic financial markets. Such supervision is important for banks that are headquartered in small economies, but operate across national borders. If such banks become so overexposed in foreign markets that a financial disruption threatens the solvency of the banks, the collapse of the banks can overwhelm domestic credit markets and outstrip the ability of the central bank to serve as the lender of last resort.

Chapter 5 - As world financial and economic leaders met January 2009 in Davos, Switzerland for the annual World Economic Forum, Switzerland's renowned flagship banks were being battered by the financial crisis and the country was facing a potentially serious economic downturn. The current financial crisis has demonstrated that financial markets in Switzerland and elsewhere have become highly interdependent and that a crisis in one market can quickly spread to other markets across national borders.

For the United States, Switzerland is important as a member of international fora where the two countries share common interests while Swiss banks also act as competitors in the international financial marketplace. One issue the two countries share concerns the organization of financial markets domestically and abroad to improve supervision and regulation of individual institutions and of international markets. This issue also focuses on developing the organizational structures within national economies that can provide oversight of the different segments of the highly complex financial system. Such oversight is viewed by many as critical, because financial markets are generally considered to play an indispensible role in allocating capital and facilitating economic activity.

In the months ahead, Members of Congress and the Obama administration likely will consider a number of proposals to restructure the supervisory and oversight responsibilities over the broad- based financial sector within the United States and in the broader international financial markets. The Swiss system provides an example of a system that has separated the regulatory and supervisory responsibilities from the monetary policy responsibilities of the Swiss National Bank and consolidated them into a national regulatory body that is subject to the Federal Council, or the executive of the Swiss government.

In: European Response to the Financial Crisis
Editor: Baron L. Whitley

ISBN: 978-1-60876-817-2
© 2010 Nova Science Publishers, Inc.

Chapter 1

COMMUNICATION FROM THE COMMISSION TO THE EUROPEAN COUNCIL: A EUROPEAN ECONOMIC RECOVERY PLAN*

Commission of the European Communities

1. INTRODUCTION

The global financial crisis has hit the EU hard. A squeeze on credit, falls in house prices and tumbling stock markets are all reinforcing a slump in consumer confidence, consumption and investment. Households are under real pressure. Businesses' order books are down. Sectors dependent on consumer credit – like private construction and the automobile industry – have seen their markets sharply deteriorate in many Member States.

The latest economic forecasts painted a bleak picture of close to zero growth and risks of contraction for the EU economy in 2009, with unemployment rising by some 2.7 million in the next two years, on the assumption that no corrective action is taken. In the weeks since the forecasts came out, economic conditions have deteriorated further:

---

* This is an edited, reformatted and augmented version of a Commission of the European Communities publication dated November 2008.

- Financial market conditions remain fragile, and are likely to be tighter for longer than expected;
- Confidence amongst households and firms has fallen much lower than expected;
- The slowdown has spread to emerging economies with negative effects for European exports.

The euro area and several Member States are already in recession. The risk is that this situation will worsen still further: that investment and consumer purchases will be put off, sparking a vicious cycle of falling demand, downsized business plans, reduced innovation, and job cuts. This could push the EU into a deep and longer-lasting recession: the economy contracting further next year, and unemployment could rise by several million people.

Quick and decisive action is needed to stop this downward spiral. Europe must use all the tools at its disposal. This means Member States and the Union working together, coordinating inside Europe and feeding into a larger global response. In tackling the financial crisis, the Union made sure that the EU level and national action worked together. This was successful in bringing stability at a time of immediate danger. Now Member States should again take advantage of the strengths of the EU – effective coordination, credible frameworks offered by the Stability and Growth Pact and the Lisbon Strategy, as well as the benefits of scale offered by the euro and the largest single market in the world. The interplay of national and EU action can help all Member States weather the worst of the global economic storms and emerge stronger from the crisis.

The euro, in particular, has proved to be an invaluable asset for the EU economies and an essential element of stability. Supported by the strong role played by the independent European Central Bank, the euro protects against destabilising exchange rate movements, which would have greatly complicated the national responses to the crisis.

A month ago, the Commission took the initiative to outline its plans for dealing with the financial crisis, addressing the difficulties of the wider economy and making Europe a key player in the global response to the financial crisis[1]. In early November, the EU's Heads of State and Government agreed on the need for a coordinated response and asked the Commission to make proposals for discussion at their December meeting.

A. European Economic Recovery Plan

This **European Economic Recovery Plan** is the Commission's response to the current economic situation. Given the scale of the crisis we are facing, the EU needs a co-ordinated approach, big enough and ambitious enough to restore consumer and business confidence. It needs to bring together all the policy levers available at EU and national level. Most of the economic policy levers, and in particular those which can stimulate consumer demand in the short term, are in the hands of the Member States. Member States have very different starting points in terms of fiscal room for manoeuvre. But that makes effective coordination all the more important.

All Member States will need to take action to deal with the crisis. Properly coordinated, national efforts can target different goals in parallel. They can cushion the blow of recession in the short term. But they can also promote the structural reforms needed to help the EU emerge stronger from the crisis, without undermining longer term fiscal sustainability. For this reason, this Recovery Plan puts particular emphasis on innovation and greening of EU investment. The EU level can act as a catalyst for such "smart action", combining EU policies and funds to help Member States maintain or pull forward investments which will create jobs, boost demand, and strengthen Europe's capacity to benefit from globalisation.

The strategic aims of the Recovery Plan are to:

- Swiftly stimulate demand and boost consumer confidence;
- Lessen the human cost of the economic downturn and its impact on the most vulnerable. Many workers and their families are or will be hit by the crisis. Action can be taken to help stem the loss of jobs; and then to help people return rapidly to the labour market, rather than face long-term unemployment;
- Help Europe to prepare to take advantage when growth returns so that the European economy is in tune with the demands of competitiveness and the needs of the future, as outlined in the Lisbon Strategy for Growth and Jobs. That means pursuing the necessary structural reforms, supporting innovation, and building a knowledge economy;
- Speed up the shift towards a low carbon economy. This will leave Europe well placed to apply its strategy for limiting climate change and promoting energy security: a strategy which will encourage new technologies, create new 'green-collar' jobs and open up new opportunities in fast growing world markets, will keep energy bills for

citizens and businesses in check, and will reduce Europe's dependence on foreign energy.

In pursuing these aims, the European Economic Recovery Plan is designed to:

- Exploit synergies and avoid negative spill-over effects through co-ordinated action;
- Draw on all available policy levers, fiscal policies, structural and financial market reforms and external action;
- Ensure full coherence between immediate actions and the EU's medium- to longer term objectives;
- Take full account of the global nature of the problem and shape the EU's contribution to international responses.

This European Economic Recovery Plan proposes a counter-cyclical macro-economic response to the crisis in the form of an ambitious set of actions to support the real economy. The aim is to avoid a deep recession. The Plan is anchored in the Stability and Growth Pact and the Lisbon Strategy for Growth and Jobs. It consists of:

- An immediate budgetary impulse amounting to € 200 bn (1.5% of EU GDP), made up of a budgetary expansion by Member States of € 170 bn (around 1.2% of EU GDP), and EU funding in support of immediate actions of the order of € 30 bn (around 0.3 % of EU GDP);
- And a number of priority actions, grounded in the Lisbon Strategy, and designed at the same time to adapt our economies to long-term challenges, continuing to implement structural reforms aimed at raising potential growth.

2. SUPPORTING THE REAL ECONOMY AND BOOSTING CONFIDENCE

As the economies of all Member States are highly integrated, sharing one single market and many common policies, any response must combine monetary and credit aspects, budgetary policy, and actions in the Lisbon strategy for growth and jobs.

2.1. Monetary and Credit Conditions

2.1.1. *The Role of the European Central Bank and other Central Banks*

In the current juncture, monetary policy has a crucial role to play. In the light of reduced inflationary expectation over the medium-term, the European Central Bank (ECB) for the euro area, along with other EU central banks, has already cut interest rates. The ECB has signalled that there is scope for further reductions. The ECB has already demonstrated its importance in stabilising markets by lending to banks and contributing to liquidity.

2.1.2. *The Role of Banks*

At the root of the problems in the real economy lies the instability in the financial markets. A reliable and efficient financial sector is a pre-requisite for a healthy, growing economy. Stabilising the banking system is therefore the first step towards halting the downturn and promoting a swift and sustainable recovery. The EU must maintain this common drive to rebuild stability and confidence in the still-fragile financial sector and create the conditions for a sustained economic recovery. The crisis has shown risks in the current governance of financial markets which have or could become real and systemic in times of serious turbulence. The pace of reform will be maintained in the coming months to restore stability and protect the interests of European citizens and business.

But it is now crucial that banks resume their normal role of providing liquidity and supporting investment in the real economy. Member States should use the major financial support provided to the banking sector to encourage a return to normal lending activities and to ensure that central interest rate cuts are passed on to borrowers. The Commission will continue to monitor the economic and competition impacts of measures taken to support the banking sector.

2.1.3. *The Role of the European Investment Bank and the European Bank for reconstruction and development*

The current crisis requires reinforced interventions from the European Investment Bank (EIB) group. The EIB will increase its yearly interventions in the EU by some €15 billion for the next two years. As this increased activity will take the form of loans, equity, guarantees and risk-sharing financing, it will also generate a positive leverage of additional investment from private sources. In total, this package proposed by EIB will help mobilise complementary private resources to support additional investments over the next two years. To enable the EIB to increase its financing activities, Member States should decide before the end of the year to incorporate EIB's reserves to reinforce its capital base in the order of € 60 bn, which will provide a highly visible political signal to the markets and which will significantly increase the Bank's lending capacity. The European Bank for Reconstruction and Development (EBRD) is also expected to add €500 million per year to its present level of financing in the new Member States.

2.2. Budgetary Policy

Restoring confidence will depend on Europe's ability to boost demand by making use of budgetary policy within the flexibility offered by the revised Stability and Growth Pact. In the current circumstances, budgetary policy has an even more important role to play in stabilising economies and sustaining demand.

Only through a significant stimulus package can Europe counter the expected downward trend in demand, with its negative knock-on effects on investments and employment. Therefore, the Commission proposes that Member States agree a co-ordinated budgetary stimulus package which should be timely, targeted and temporary, to be implemented immediately.

In the context of national budgets for 2009, this co-ordinated budgetary impulse should be € 170 bn, which represents 1.2% of the Union's GDP, in order to produce a substantive positive and rapid impact on the European economy and on employment, in addition to the role of the automatic stabilisers. Expenditures and/or reductions in taxation included in the budgetary impulse should be consistent with the flexibility offered by the Stability and Growth Pact and reinforce the structural reforms of the Lisbon Strategy. This budgetary stimulus should be temporary. Member States should commit to reverse the budgetary deterioration and return to the aims set out in the medium term objectives.

To maximise its impact, the budgetary stimulus should take account of the starting positions of each Member State. It is clear that not all Member States are in the same position. Those that took advantage of the good times to achieve more sustainable public finance positions and improve their competitive positions have more room for manoeuvre now. For those Member States, in particular outside the euro area, which are facing significant external and internal imbalances, budgetary policy should essentially aim at correcting such imbalances.

This budgetary stimulus must be well designed and be based on the following principles:

(1) It should be timely, temporary, targeted, and co-ordinated
National budgetary stimulus packages should be:

- *timely* so that they quickly support economic activity during the period of low demand, as delays in implementation could mean that the fiscal impulse only comes when the recovery is underway;

- *temporary* so as to avoid a permanent deterioration in budgetary positions which would undermine sustainability and eventually require financing through sustained future tax increases;

- *targeted* towards the source of the economic challenge (increasing unemployment, credit constrained firms/households, etc. and supporting structural reforms) as this maximises the stabilisation impact of limited budgetary resources;

- *co-ordinated* so that they multiply the positive impact and ensure long term budgetary sustainability.

(2) It should mix revenue and expenditure instruments
In general, discretionary public spending is considered to have a stronger positive impact on demand in the short-run compared with tax cuts. This is because some consumers may prefer to save rather than spend, unless the tax cuts are limited in time. Taking the different situations of Member States into account the following measures could be considered[2]:

- *Public expenditure* has an impact on demand in the short-term. Measures that can be introduced quickly and targeted at households which are especially hard hit by the slowdown are likely to feed through almost directly to consumption, e.g temporarily increased transfers to the unemployed or low income households, or a temporary lengthening of the duration of unemployment benefit. This can also be done through frontloading public investment in projects which could benefit SMEs and could support long-term public policy goals such as improving infrastructure endowments or tackling climate change;

- *Guarantees and loan subsidies to compensate for the unusually high current risk premium* can be particularly effective in an environment where credit is generally constrained. They can help bridge a lack of short-term of working capital which is currently a problem for many companies;

- *Well designed financial incentives* for speeding up the adaptation of our economies to long-term challenges such as climate change, including for example incentives for energy efficiency;

- *Lower taxes and social contributions:* lower social contributions paid by employers can have a positive impact on job retention and creation while lower taxation of labour income can support purchasing power in particular for low wage earners;

- *Temporary reductions* in the level of the standard rate of VAT can be introduced quickly and might provide a fiscal impulse to support consumption.

(3) It should be conducted within the stability and growth pact

Budgetary policy should be conducted within the Stability and Growth Pact, so as to provide a common and credible framework for policy. The 2005 revision of the Pact allows better account to be taken of cyclical conditions while strengthening medium and long-term fiscal discipline. The resulting framework is more demanding in good times, it affords more flexibility in bad times. Extraordinary circumstances combining a financial crisis and a recession justify a co-ordinated budgetary expansion in the EU. It may lead some Member States to breach the 3% GDP deficit reference value. For Member States considered to be in an excessive deficit, corrective action will have to be taken in time frames consistent with the recovery of the economy. This is fully consistent with the procedures of the Stability and Growth Pact which guarantee that the excessive deficit will be corrected in due time, ensuring long-term sustainability of the budgetary positions.

The Stability and Growth Pact will therefore be applied judiciously ensuring credible medium-term fiscal policy strategies. Member States putting in place counter-cyclical measures should submit an updated Stability or Convergence Programme by the end of December 2008. This update should spell out the measures that will be put in place to reverse the fiscal deterioration and ensure long-term sustainability. The Commission will then assess the budgetary impulse measures and stability and convergence programmes based on updated forecasts and will provide guidance on the appropriate stance, relying on the following objectives:

- ensuring the reversibility of measures increasing deficits in the short term;
- improving budgetary policy-making in the medium-term, through a strengthening of the national budgetary rules and frameworks;
- ensuring long-term sustainability of public finances, in particular through reforms curbing the rise in age-related expenditure.

(4) It should be accompanied by structural reforms that support demand and promote resilience

While the most immediate impact on growth and jobs in the short run needs to come from a monetary and fiscal stimulus, a comprehensive recovery plan also needs to encompass an ambitious **structural reform agenda** tailored to the needs of individual Member States, and designed to equip them to emerge stronger from the crisis. In part, this is because some structural reforms can also contribute to bolstering aggregate demand in the short term. Moreover, structural reforms are necessary to address some of the underlying root causes of the present crisis, as well as to strengthen the economy's adjustment capacity needed for a rapid recovery.

A resilient, flexible economy helps mitigate the adverse impact of an economic crisis. The Lisbon Strategy has already strengthened the European economic fundamentals. Appropriately tailored, Lisbon strategy structural reforms could be an appropriate short-term policy response to the crisis as they strengthen economic resilience and flexibility. Member States should consider the following measures:

- *Supporting consumer purchasing power through improved market functioning:* policies that improve the functioning of key markets can help sustain demand by helping bring down prices, thus supporting the purchasing power of households;

- *Addressing immediate competitiveness problems.* In Member States with inflation and competitiveness problems measures need to be taken urgently that reinforce the link between the wage setting mechanism and productivity developments;

- *Supporting employment and facilitating labour market transitions*: today's prime labour market challenge is to avoid wasteful labour shedding by industries temporarily affected by short-term demand disturbances. To that end, more flexibility in working time arrangements or enhanced employment services could help;

- *Reducing regulatory and administrative burdens on businesses.* Such reforms help increase productivity, and strengthen competitiveness. Measures that can be implemented rapidly include continuing efforts to reduce the time to start up a business.

2.3. Actions in the Four Priority Areas of the Lisbon Strategy

In order to produce maximum benefits and achieve the Recovery Plan's aims of protecting people and preventing the crisis from deflecting attention from the EU's longer-term interests and the need to invest in its future, there should be a close connection between the fiscal stimulus and actions in the four priority areas of the Lisbon Strategy (people, business, infrastructure and energy, research and innovation), as outlined in this section. In order to achieve this, as part of its annual Lisbon package, the Commission will issue individual reports for each Member State on 16 December 2008 which will include proposals for recommendations.

A smart combination of EU policies and funds can act as a catalyst for key investments taking the EU in the direction of future sustainable prosperity. It is equally important to provide for stable foreseeable framework conditions to boost confidence, facilitate investment and to work for least cost solutions to common problems. Some of the actions proposed in this section are designed to frontload EU funding directly to contribute to the fiscal stimulus and assist Member States with the implementation of their policies. Others are intended to improve the framework conditions for future investments, reduce administrative burdens and speed up innovation. Overall, the actions form an integrated package: their budgetary implications should take into account the principles set out in the previous section.

2.3.1. *Protecting Employment and Promoting Entrepreneurship*

The top priority must be to protect Europe's citizens from the worst effects of the financial crisis. They are the first to be hit whether as workers, households, or as entrepreneurs. In addressing the employment and social impact of the financial crisis, Member States should actively involve the social partners.

(a) People

The implementation of active inclusion and integrated flexicurity policies, focused on activation measures, re-training and skills upgrading, are essential to promote employability, ensure rapid re-integration into the labour market of workers who have been made redundant and avoid long term unemployment. Within this context, adequate social protection that provides incentives to work whilst preserving purchasing power will also be important.

1. Launch a major European employment support initiative

(a) The Commission is proposing to simplify criteria for European Social Fund (ESF) support and step up advance payments from early 2009, so that Member States have earlier access to up to € 1.8 bn in order to:

- Within flexicurity strategies, rapidly **reinforce activation schemes**, in particular for the low-skilled, involving personalised counselling, intensive (re-)training and upskilling of workers, apprenticeships, subsidised employment as well as grants for self-employment, business start-up's and
- Refocus their programmes to **concentrate support on the most vulnerable**, and where necessary opt for full Community financing of projects during this period;
- Improve the monitoring and **matching of skills** development and upgrading with existing and anticipated job vacancies; this will be implemented in close cooperation with social partners, public employment services and universities;

Working with Member States, the Commission proposes to re-programme ESF expenditure to ensure that immediate priorities are met.

(b) The Commission will also propose to revise the rules of the European Globalisation Adjustment Fund so that it can intervene more rapidly in key sectors, either to co- finance training and job placements for those who are made redundant or to keep in the labour market skilled workers who will be needed once the economy starts to recover. The Commission will review the budgetary means available for the Fund in the light of the implementation of the revised rules.

2. Create demand for labour

- Member States should consider reducing employers' social charges on lower incomes to promote the employability of lower skilled workers. Member States should also consider the introduction of innovative solutions (e.g. service cheques for household and child care, temporary hiring subsidies for vulnerable groups), which have already been successfully pioneered in parts of the Union;
- The Council should adopt, before the 2009 Spring European Council, the proposed directive to make permanent **reduced VAT rates for labour-intensive services**.

(b) Business

Sufficient and affordable access to finance is a pre-condition for investment, growth and job creation by the private sector. Member States need to use the leverage they have through the provision of major financial support to the banking sector to ensure that banks resume their normal lending activities. To support small businesses and entrepreneurship, the EU and Member States must take urgent steps to substantially reduce administrative burdens for SMEs and micro-enterprises, in particular by fast-tracking the corresponding Commission's proposals. To this end, the European Small Business Act should also be implemented as soon as possible.

The EU's state aid rules offer Member States a wide range of possibilities for providing financial support to companies, regions and workers/the unemployed and to stimulate demand. At the same time these rules guarantee a level playing field, ensuring that state aids are used to support EU objectives such as R&D, innovation, ICT, transport and energy efficiency, and not to unduly distort competition by favouring particular companies or sectors. In the current exceptional circumstances, access to finance is a major business concern and the Commission will develop temporary guidelines allowing state support for loans (see below).

3. Enhance access to financing for business

- The EIB has put together a package of € 30 bn for loans to SME's, an increase by € 10 billion over its usual lending in this sector;
- The EIB will also reinforce by € 1 bn a year its **lending to mid-sized corporations**, a key sector of the EU economy. Furthermore, an additional € 1 billion will be conferred by the EIB to the EIF for a mezzanine finance facility;
- The Commission will put in place a **simplification package**, notably to **speed up its State aid decision-making**. Any state aid should be channelled through horizontal schemes designed to promote the Lisbon objectives, notably research, innovation, training, environmental protection and in particular clean technologies, transport and energy efficiency. The Commission will **temporarily authorise Member States to ease access to finance for companies** through subsidised guarantees and loan subsidies for investments in products going beyond EU environmental standards[3]

4. Reduce administrative burdens and promote entrepreneurship

Building on the Small Business Act, and in order significantly **reduce administrative burdens on business**, promote their cash flow and help more people to become entrepreneurs, the EU and Member States should:

- Ensure that starting up a business anywhere in the EU can be done within three days at zero costs and that formalities for the hiring of the first employee can be fulfilled via a single access point;
- Remove the requirement on **micro-enterprises** to prepare annual accounts (the estimated savings for these companies are € 7bn per year) and limit the capital requirements of the European private company to one euro;
- Accelerate the adoption of the **European private company** statute proposal so that from early 2009 it can facilitate cross border business activities of SMEs and to allow them to work under a single set of corporate rules across the EU;
- Ensure that public authorities **pay invoices**, including to SMEs, for supplies and services within one month to ease liquidity constraints and accept e-invoicing as equivalent to paper invoicing (this could deliver cost reductions of up to 18 € Bn); any arrears

owed by public bodies should also be settled;
- Reduce by up to 75% the fees for **patent applications** and maintenance and halve the costs for an EU trademark.

2.3.2. Continuing to Invest in the Future

We are witnessing the beginning of a major structural shift towards a low carbon economy. This provides the EU with an opportunity that will create new businesses, new industries and millions of new well-paying jobs. All sectors must participate: for example, the recent decision on the CAP health check commits €3 Bn for climate-friendly investments in rural development. This is where short-term action can bring immediate as well as lasting benefits to the Union. To accelerate investments, the Commission will clarify the legal framework for partnerships between the public and private sector aiming at carrying out major infrastructure and research investments, in order to facilitate this mixed mode of financing.

(c) Infrastructure and Energy

The key to maximising benefits and minimising costs is to target opportunities to boost energy efficiency, for example, of buildings, lighting, cooling and heating systems, and of other technologies like vehicles and machinery. Major positive effects for households and businesses can be harvested in the short term.

At the same time, Europe needs to accelerate its investments in infrastructure, particularly in the environmentally-friendly transport-modes which are part of the Trans-European Networks (TENs), high-speed ICT networks, energy interconnections, and pan-European research infrastructures. Speeding up infrastructure investments will not only cushion the blow to the construction sector, which is slowing down sharply in most Member States, it will also enhance Europe's longer-term sustainable growth-potential. Particularly in the energy sector a number of high profile trans-European projects would help to increase the EU's energy security and integrate more Member States into the European electricity grid.

5. Step up investments to modernise Europe's infrastructure

- For at least the next two years, the EU budget is unlikely to spend the full amount set out in the financial framework. Therefore, for 2009 and 2010, the Commission proposes to mobilise an

additional € 5 bn for trans-European energy interconnections and broadband infrastructure projects. To make this happen, Council and Parliament will need to agree to revise the financial framework, while remaining within the limits of the current budget;

- With a financial envelope of over € 347 bn for 2007-2013, cohesion policy provides considerable support to public investment by Member States and regions. However, there is a risk that pressure on national budgets will slow down the rate of planned investment. To give an immediate boost to the economy, **the implementation of the structural funds should be accelerated.** To this end:
  - The Commission will propose to increase its pre-financing of programmes to make up to € 4.5 bn available earlier in 2009;
  - Member States should use the available flexibility to frontload the financing of projects by enhancing the part financed by the Community;
  - The Commission will propose a number of other measures designed to bring forward the implementation of major investment projects, to facilitate the use of financial engineering funds, to simplify the treatment of advances paid to the beneficiaries and to widen the possibilities for eligible expenditure on a flat rate basis for all the funds.

The Commission underlines the need for early adoption of these proposals.

- By the end of March 2009 the Commission will launch a €500 million call for proposals for **trans-European transport (TEN-T) projects** where this money would lead to construction beginning before the end of 2009. This will bring forward existing funds that would have been reallocated by the mid-term review of the multi-annual TEN-T programme in 2010;
- In parallel, the EIB will significantly increase its financing of climate change, energy security and infrastructure investments by up to € 6 bn per year, while also accelerating the implementation of the two innovative financial instruments jointly developed with the Commission, i.e. the Risk Sharing Finance Facility to support R&D and the Loan Guarantee Instrument for TEN-T projects to

stimulate greater participation of the private sector;
- The EBRD will more than double its efforts for energy efficiency, climate change mitigation and financing for municipalities and other infrastructure services. This could lead through the mobilisation of private sector financing to € 5 bn investments.

6. Improve energy efficiency in buildings

Acting together, Member States and EU Institutions should take urgent measures to improve the energy efficiency of the housing stock and public buildings and promote rapid take up of 'green' products:

- Member States should set demanding targets for ensuring that public buildings and both private and social housing meet the highest European **energy-efficiency** standards and make them subject to energy certification on a regular basis. To facilitate reaching their national targets, Member States should consider introducing a reduction of property tax for energy-performing buildings. The Commission has just tabled proposals[4] for a major upgrading in the energy efficiency of buildings and calls on the Council and Parliament to give priority to their adoption;
- In addition, Member States should **re-programme their structural funds** operational programmes' to devote a greater share to energy-efficiency investments, including where they fund social housing. To widen possibilities, the Commission is proposing an amendment to the Structural Funds Regulations to support this move and stresses the need for early adoption of the amendments;
- The Commission will work with the EIB and a number of national development banks to launch a **2020 fund for energy, climate change and infrastructure** to fund equity and quasi-equity projects;
- The Commission calls on Member States and industry urgently to develop **innovative financing models**, for example, where refurbishments are financed through repayments, based on savings made on energy bills, over several years.

7. Promote the rapid take-up of "green products"

- The Commission will propose **reduced VAT rates for green**

products and services, aimed at improving in particular **energy efficiency of buildings**. It encourages Member States to provide further incentives to consumers to stimulate demand for environmentally-friendly products;
- In addition, Member States should rapidly **implement environmental performance** requirements for external power supplies, stand-by and off mode electric power consumption, set top boxes and fluorescent lamps;
- The Commission will urgently draw up measures for **other products which offer very high potential for energy savings** such as televisions, domestic lighting, refrigerators and freezers, washing machines, boilers and air-conditioners.

(d) Research and Innovation

The financial crisis and the subsequent squeeze on financial resources, both public and private, may tempt some to delay, or substantially cut, planned R&D and education investments, as has happened in the past when Europe was hit by a downturn. With hindsight, such decisions amounted to a major capital and knowledge destruction with very negative effects for Europe's growth and employment prospects in the medium to longer-term. However, there have also been examples of countries, both inside and outside Europe, which had the foresight to increase R&D and education expenditure in difficult economic times, by which they laid the basis for their strong position in innovation.

8. Increase investment in R&D, Innovation and Education

Member States and the private sector should increase planned investments in education and R&D (consistent with **their national R&D targets**) to stimulate growth and productivity. They should also consider ways to **increase private sector R&D investments**, for example, by providing fiscal incentives, grants and/or subsidies. Member States should maintain investments to increase the quality of education.

9. Developing clean technologies for cars and construction.

To **support innovation in manufacturing, in particular in the construction industry and the automobile sector** which have recently seen demand plummet as a result of the crisis and which also face significant challenges in the transition to the green economy, the Commission proposes to launch **3 major partnerships between the** public and private sectors:

- **In the automobile sector, a 'European green cars initiative'**, involving research on a broad range of technologies and smart energy infrastructures essential to achieve a breakthrough in the use of renewable and non-polluting energy sources, safety and traffic fluidity. The partnership would be funded by the Community, the EIB, industry and Member States' contributions with a combined envelope of at least € 5 bn. In this context, the EIB would provide cost-based loans to car producers and suppliers to finance innovation, in particular in technologies improving the safety and the environmental performance of cars, e.g. electric vehicles. Demand side measures such as a reduction by Member States of their registration and circulation taxes for lower emission cars, as well as efforts to scrap old cars, should be integrated into the initiative. In addition, the Commission will support the development of a procurement network of regional and local authorities to pool demand for clean buses and other vehicles and speed up the implementation of the CARS2 1 initiative;
- **In the construction sector, a 'European energy-efficient buildings' initiative**, to promote green technologies and the development of energy-efficient systems and materials in new and renovated buildings with a view to reducing radically their energy consumption and CO_2 emissions[5]. The initiative should have an important regulatory and standardisation component and would involve a procurement network of regional and local authorities. The estimated envelope for this partnership is € 1bn. The initiative would be backed by specific actions proposed under actions 5 and 6 on infrastructure and energy-efficiency;
- **To increase the use of technology in manufacturing, "a factories of the future initiative"**: The objective is to help EU manufacturers across sectors, in particular SMEs, to adapt to global competitive pressures by increasing the technological base of EU manufacturing through the development and integration the enabling technologies of the future, such as engineering technologies for adaptable machines and industrial processes, ICT, and advanced materials. The estimated envelope for this action is € 1.2 bn.

10. High-speed Internet for all

High-speed Internet connections promote rapid technology diffusion, which in turn creates demand for innovative products and services. Equipping Europe with this modern infrastructure is as important as building the railways in the nineteenth century. To boost Europe's lead in fixed and wireless communications and accelerate the development of high value-added services, the Commission and Member States should work with stakeholders to develop a **broadband strategy** to accelerate the up-grading and extension of networks. The strategy will be supported by public funds in order to provide broadband access to under-served and high cost areas where the market cannot deliver. The aim should be to reach 100% coverage of high speed internet by 2010. In addition, and also with a view to upgrading the performance of existing networks, Member States should promote competitive investments in fibre networks and endorse the Commission's proposals to free up spectrum for wireless broadband. Using the funding mentioned in action 5 above, the Commission will channel an additional € 1 bn to these network investments in 2009/10.

3. WORKING TOWARDS GLOBAL SOLUTIONS

The challenges the EU is now facing are part of the global macro economic challenges highlighted by the recent Summit on Financial Markets and the World Economy in Washington. This European Economic Recovery Plan will form part of the EU's contribution to closer international macro economic co-operation, including with emerging countries, designed to restore growth, avoid negative spillovers and support developing countries. The EU has benefited greatly in recent decades from increased cross-border capital and trade flows with developed countries and increasingly also with emerging economies. The financial crisis has shown just how interdependent the world has become. The scale and speed at which a loss of confidence in one part of the world soon affected financial markets and spilt over to real economies worldwide is rightly a matter of concern. In today's world, a shock to one systemically important financial market is a global problem and has to be treated accordingly. So a key part of any co-ordinated EU response to the economic downturn will have to come through greater engagement with our international partners, and with international organisations, working together to tackle challenges at home and abroad, including in developing countries which will be among those hardest hit.

Keeping World Trade Moving

Europe's recovery depends on our companies' ability to make best use of the possibilities that global markets offer. Europe's return to solid growth will also depend on its capacity to export. Keeping trade links and investment opportunities open is also the best means to limit the global impact of the crisis, since global recovery will depend crucially on the sustainable economic performance of emerging and developing economies.

We must therefore maintain our commitment to open markets across the globe, keeping our own market as open as possible and insisting that third countries do the same, in particular by ensuring compliance with WTO rules. To reach this objective Europe should take renewed action to:

- Reach early agreement on a **global trade deal** in the WTO Doha Round. Following the renewed commitment made at the 15 November Washington Summit, the Commission has immediately stepped up efforts with key WTO partners to reach an agreement on modalities by the end of the year. A successful Round will send a strong short-term signal of confidence in the new global economic order. Over time it will bring consumers and businesses all over the world benefits in terms of lower prices, by cutting remaining high tariffs in key partner markets;
- Continue to support the economic and social consolidation of the candidate countries and the **Western Balkans** in the mutual interest of the EU and the region. To this end the Commission will put in place a € 120 million "Crisis Response Package" leveraging an amount of € 500 million in loans from International Financial Institutions;
- **Create a network of deep and comprehensive free trade agreements** in its neighbourhood as a step towards a more integrated regional market. Working through its neighbourhood policy, the EU can build on the Union for the Mediterranean and its plans for a new Eastern Partnership;
- Step up efforts to secure new and ambitious **Free Trade Agreements** with other trade partners;

- Build a close working relationship with the new US administration, including through the **Transatlantic Economic Council**. More effective regulatory cooperation could also be pursued with other key industrialised countries, such as Canada and Japan;
- Continue **dialogues with key bilateral partners** such as China, India, Brazil and Russia and use them to address public procurement, competition and intellectual property issues.

Tackling Climate Change

The crisis is occurring on the eve of a major structural shift towards the low carbon economy. The goal of fighting climate change can be combined with major new economic opportunities to develop new technologies and create jobs and enhance energy security.

Agreement in the December European Council and with the European Parliament on the EU's internal climate change strategy will strengthen the leading role the EU must seek to play in securing an ambitious international agreement on climate change at the UNFCCC conference in Copenhagen at the end of 2009.

Supporting Developing Countries

The current crisis will further add to existing pressures on developing countries, which are often least well positioned to cope. So it is all the more important that the EU, and others, maintain their commitments to achieving the Millennium Development Goals (MDG). It may also be necessary for developed countries and regions, like the EU, to come up with new, flexible and innovative instruments to help developing countries face the rapid impact of the crisis such as the EU's recent food aid facility.

Continuing to help emerging and developing countries on the path to sustainable growth is particularly relevant in the run up to the International Conference on Financing for Development, which will take place in Doha from 29 November – 2 December. At this meeting, the EU – which in 2007 continued to be the largest donor of Overseas Development Assistance (ODA) - will reaffirm its commitment to arriving at ODA target levels of 0.5 6% of

GNP by 2010 and 0.7% by 2015. It will also invite other donors to continue to work towards these goals.

Supporting sustainable development, *inter alia* through delivering on ODA targets and MDG goals, but also through addressing overall governance challenges, is all the more important in times of economic crisis. Sharing the benefits of sustainable growth, tackling climate change, energy and food security and good governance, are interlinked challenges, where international financial institutions, like other international bodies, also have an important role to play.

4. Conclusions

It is clear that the EU faces a difficult time in the coming months as the effects of the world and European economic slow down puts pressure on jobs and demand. But, acting together, Member States and European Institutions can take action to restore consumer and business confidence, to restart lending and stimulate investment in our economies, creating jobs and helping the unemployed to find new jobs. **The European Economic Recovery Plan** set out in this Communication is designed to create a basis for rapid agreement between Member States to get Europe's economy moving again.

The European Commission calls on the European Parliament to lend its full support to this European Economic Recovery Plan.

It calls on Heads of State and Government, at their meeting on 11 and 12 December 2008, to:

(1) Endorse this European Economic Recovery Plan;
(2) Request the European Commission and the Council to work together to ensure that combined national and EU level measures amount to at least 1.5% of GDP;
(3) Ensure that updated Stability and Convergence Programmes including the national impulse measures, are assessed in accordance with the procedures laid down in the Stability and Growth Pact, while making use of the flexibility it offers;
(4) Endorse the 10 actions outlined in the European Economic Recovery Plan; urge the Council and Parliament to accelerate any legislative activity needed to implement these measures;

(5) Agree, on the basis of a Commission contribution before the 2009 Spring European Council assessing progress made with the implementation of the Plan, to identify any further measures necessary at EU and Member State level to stimulate the recovery;

(6) Continue to work closely with international partners to implement global solutions to strengthen global governance and promote the economic recovery.

End Notes

[1] Communication of 29 October - COM(2008) 706.

[2] The general recommendations and the specific actions related to the priority areas set out in this document are subject to compliance with internal market and competition rules, notably for State aid.

[3] This will be done by raising the current €1.5 M safe harbour threshold for risk capital to € 2.5M, and by allowing, subject to certain conditions and maximum amounts, (a) to grant aid for guarantees for loans for certain companies having difficulties to obtain loans; and (b) to grant aid of up to 50% (for SMEs and 25% (for large companies) of the Reference Rate, for loans for investments in the manufacture of products complying earlier with, or going beyond, new Community standards which increase the level of environmental protection and are not yet in force.

[4] COM(2008) 755, 13.11.2008.

[5] Buildings currently account for 40% of energy consumption.

In: European Response to the Financial Crisis ISBN: 978-1-60876-817-2
Editor: Baron L. Whitley © 2010 Nova Science Publishers, Inc.

Chapter 2

THE FINANCIAL CRISIS: IMPACT ON AND RESPONSE BY THE EUROPEAN UNION[*]

James K. Jackson

SUMMARY

According to the most recent National Threat Assessment, the global financial crisis and its geopolitical implications pose the primary near-term security concern of the United States. Over the short run, both the EU and the United States are attempting to resolve the financial crisis while stimulating domestic demand to stem the economic downturn. These efforts have born little progress so far as the economic recession and the financial crisis have become reinforcing events, causing EU governments to forge policy responses to both crises. In addition, both the United States and the EU likely will confront the prospect of growing economic and political instability in Eastern Europe and elsewhere over the impact of the economic recession on restive populations. In the long run, the United States and the EU likely will search for a regulatory scheme that provides for greater stability while not inadvertently offering advantages to any one country or group. Throughout the crisis, the European Central Bank and other central banks have assumed a critical role as the primary institutions with the necessary political and

---

[*] This is an edited, reformatted and augmented version of a Congressional Research Service Report R40415, dated June 24, 2009.

economic clout to respond effectively. Within Europe, national governments, private firms, and international organizations have varied in their response to the financial crisis, reflecting differing views over the proper policy course to pursue and the unequal effects of the financial crisis and the economic downturn. Initially, some EU members preferred to address the crisis on a case-by-case basis. As the crisis has persisted, however, leaders have begun looking for a systemic approach that ultimately may affect the drive within Europe toward greater economic integration.

Within the United States, Congress has appropriated funds to help recapitalize financial institutions, and adopted several economic stimulus measures. In addition, Congress likely will be involved in efforts to reshape institutions and frameworks for international cooperation and coordination in financial markets. European governments are also adopting fiscal measures to stimulate their economies and wrestling with failing banks. The financial crisis has demonstrated that financial markets are highly interdependent and that extensive networks link financial markets across national borders, which is pressing EU governments to work together to find a mutually reinforcing solution. Unlike the United States, however, where the federal government can legislate policies that are consistent across all 50 States, the EU process gives each EU member a great deal of discretion to decide how they will regulate and supervise financial markets within their borders. The limits of this system may well be tested as the EU and others search for a regulatory framework that spans a broad number of national markets. Governments that have expended considerable resources utilizing fiscal and monetary policy tools to stabilize the financial system and to provided a boost to their economies may be required to be increasingly more inventive in providing yet more stimulus to their economies and face political unrest in domestic populations. Attention likely will also focus on those governments that are viewed as not expending economic resources commensurate with the size of their economies to stimulate economic growth

OVERVIEW

Some members of the European Union[1] (EU) initially viewed the financial crisis as a purely American phenomenon. That view has changed as economic activity in the EU has declined at a fast pace over a short period of time. Making matters worse, global trade has declined sharply, eroding prospects for

European exports providing a safety valve for domestic industries that are cutting output. In addition, public protests, sparked by rising rates of unemployment and concerns over the growing financial and economic turmoil, are increasing the political stakes for EU governments and their leaders. The global economic crisis is straining the ties that bind together the members of the EU and could present a significant challenge to the ideals of solidarity and common interests. In addition, the longer the economic downturn persists, the greater the prospects are that international pressure will mount against those governments that are perceived as not carrying their share of the responsibility for stimulating their economies to an extent that is commensurate with the size of their economy. According to Dennis Blair, Director of U.S. National Intelligence, the global financial crisis and its geopolitical implications pose, "the primary near-term security concern of the United States." In addition, he said, "The longer it takes for the [economic] recovery to begin, the greater the likelihood of serious damage to U.S. strategic interests. Roughly a quarter of the countries in the world have already experienced low- level instability such as government changes because of the current slowdown."[2]

Various EU governments have had to expend public resources to rescue failing banks, in addition to protecting depositors and utilizing monetary and fiscal tools to support banks, to unfreeze credit markets, and to stimulate economic growth. These efforts have born modest progress so far as the economic recession and the financial crisis have become reinforcing events, which are forcing EU governments to forge policy responses to both crises. As the loss of real and financial wealth worsens, EU governments have worked both independently and in concert to address the immediate requirements of protecting financial institutions and improving access to credit by households and businesses. The differential effects of the economic downturn, however, are dividing the wealthier countries of the Eurozone[3] from the poorer countries within the EU and in East Europe and are compounding efforts to respond to the financial crisis and the economic recession. Once the immediate issues are resolved, EU governments likely will address long-term solutions to regulating and supervising financial markets. EU governments have found some common ground for solutions to the financial crisis, but the financial crisis has demonstrated that the international scope of financial activities often cause firms operating in their respective jurisdictions to compete over the highly lucrative financial services sector. In the long run, they likely will search for a regulatory scheme that provides for greater stability while not inadvertently offering advantages to any one group.

For the United States and the members of the European Union the stakes are high. Over the short run, both the EU and the United States are attempting to stop the downward spiral in the financial system, improve the financial architecture, and restore balanced economic growth. Over the long run, they likely will search for a regulatory scheme that provides for greater stability while not inadvertently offering advantages to any one country. The financial crisis and the economic downturn have become global events and likely will dominate the attention of policymakers for some time to come. Governments that have expended considerable resources utilizing fiscal and monetary policy tools to stabilize the financial system and to provide a boost to their economies may be required to be increasingly more inventive in providing yet more stimulus to their economies and face political unrest in domestic populations.

EU members are also concerned over the impact the financial crisis and the economic recession are having on the economies of East Europe and prospects for political instability[4] as well as future prospects for market reforms. Worsening economic conditions in East European countries could compound the current problems facing financial institutions in EU members. While mutual necessity may eventually dictate a more unified position among EU members and increased efforts to aid East European economies, some observers are concerned these actions may come too late to forestall another blow to the EU economies and to the United States. Governments elsewhere in Europe, such as Iceland and Latvia, have collapsed as a result of public protests over the way their governments have handled their economies during the crisis, and the International Monetary Fund has issued emergency loans to Hungary ($15.7 billion) and Ukraine ($16.4 billion). In addition, the IMF has issued loans to Belarus (2.48 billion), Bosnia and Herzegovina ($1.52 billion), Iceland ($2.1 billion), Latvia ($2.35 billion), Moldova ($118.2 million), Poland ($20.58 billion), Romania ($17.1 billion), and Serbia ($4.0 billion). The World Bank in a joint effort with the European Bank for Reconstruction and Development and the European Investment Bank announced on February 27, 2009 that they were providing $31 billion over two years to assist ailing banks and businesses in Eastern and Central Europe.[5]

East European countries are experiencing a sharp depreciation in their currencies relative to the Euro and the economic crisis likely will cause their government deficits to rise, undermining the efforts of some of the countries to join the Eurozone.[6] Banks in the EU have nearly $1.5 trillion in assets potentially at risk in Central and Eastern Europe. The data in **Table 1** include the exposure of the major Western European banks for East European countries and the Russian Federation. Despite this exposure to banks in

Eastern Europe, EU leaders, at a meeting on March 1, 2009 reportedly could not agree on a common approach to the financial crisis and rejected a call by Hungary for financial support for Eastern Europe. Even the East European participants could not bridge their differences and present a unified approach to the EU. Some East European countries pushed for substantial financial assistance from the EU, while other countries expressed little interest in receiving financial assistance.[7]

The crisis has underscored the growing interdependence between financial markets and between the U.S. and European economies. As such, the synchronized nature of the current economic downturn probably means that neither the United States nor the EU is likely to emerge from the financial crisis or the economic downturn alone. The United States and the EU share a mutual interest in developing a sound financial architecture to improve supervision and regulation of individual institutions and of international markets. This issue includes developing the organization and structures within national economies that can provide oversight of the different segments of the highly complex financial system. This oversight is viewed by many as critical to the future of the financial system because financial markets generally are considered to play an indispensible role in allocating capital and facilitating economic activity.

In the months ahead, Congress and the Obama Administration likely will consider a number of proposals to restructure the supervisory and regulatory responsibilities over the broad-based financial sector within the United States. At the same time, such international organizations, as the G-20, the Financial Stability Forum, the International Monetary Fund, the Organization for Economic Cooperation and Development, and the Bank for International Settlements likely will offer their own prescriptions for the international financial markets.

Financial Architecture

As policymakers address the issue of financial supervision, they likely will weigh the costs and benefits of centralizing supervisory responsibilities into a few key entities, such as the Federal Reserve, or dispersing them more widely across a number of different entities. A centralized approach may avoid the haphazard way in which certain complex financial markets and transactions went largely unregulated. On the other hand, a broader dispersion of supervisory responsibilities may yield a more specialized approach to market supervision. In the United States, the Federal Reserve holds a monopoly over the conduct of monetary policy, mainly as a means of keeping such policy-making independent of political interests. The Federal Reserve also shares regulatory and supervisory responsibilities with a number of different agencies that are more directly accountable to elected officials and are subject to change. The EU system, however, is different from the U.S. system in ways that may complicate efforts at coordination. For instance, the European Central Bank is not strictly comparable to the Federal Reserve in both scope of its regulatory role and its role in supervising banks. In the EU system each EU member has its own institutional and legal framework for regulating its banking market, and national supervisory authorities are organized differently by each EU country with different powers and accountability.

On various occasions over the past several months, EU leaders have discussed the need to develop a common set of rules that could help regulate financial markets and prevent another financial crisis. What has emerged, however, is a lack of consensus over the details of such a regulatory scheme. On February 22, 2009, leaders and Finance Ministers from Germany, the United Kingdom, France, Italy, Spain, the Netherlands, Czech Republic, and Luxembourg met in Berlin to map out a common approach to overhauling financial rules in preparation for the G20 meeting in London on April 2, 2009. A position paper prepared by German Finance Minister Peer Steinbruck set out five areas of discussion for the European leaders: 1) transparency and accountability; 2) enhancing "sound regulation; 3) promoting integrity in financial markets; 4) strengthening international cooperation; and 5) reforming international financial institutions. Beyond these vague goals, the group has not been able to provide a detailed roadmap of how to achieve a new financial architecture, or to gain a unified approach within the broader membership of the EU.

The European leaders also considered proposals for the G20 meeting that would require banks to increase their capital resources in periods of faster economic growth. Reportedly, the Ministers also discussed the growing economic problems in Eastern European countries, tax havens, trade protectionism, and a $500 billion fund for the International Monetary Fund to deal with economic crises. Following the formal talks, German Chancellor Merkel spoke in favor of adopting global regulations for financial markets and hedge funds. In a statement released on behalf of all of the leaders, Chancellor Merkel said, "All financial markets, products, and participants, including hedge funds and other private pools of capital which may pose a systemic risk must be subjected to appropriate oversight or regulation."[8]

Table 1. Major Western European Banks' Claims on Central and Eastern Europe

	Austria	Belgium	France	Germany	Italy	Netherlands	Sweden	Total
Belarus	$2.1	$0.1	$0.2	$0.9	$0.2	$0.1	$0.0	$3.6
Bulgaria	5.7	2.0	3.6	2.8	8.1	0.7	0.0	22.9
Czech. Rep.	65.1	56.7	38.6	12.7	19.0	6.2	0.2	198.5
Estonia	0.3	0.1	0.1	1.1	0.4	0.0	32.7	34.7
Hungary	38.3	18.7	11.9	37.9	29.3	5.6	0.3	142.0
Latvia	0.8	0.0	0.4	4.8	1.4	0.0	25.0	32.4
Lithuania	0.3	0.1	0.4	3.8	0.7	0.0	28.9	34.2
Poland	17.2	25.2	22.9	55.4	54.4	41.2	8.1	224.4
Romania	46.5	1.2	17.6	3.8	12.9	11.0	0.2	93.2
Russian Fed.	23.9	10.3	34.7	49.5	25.7	25.5	9.9	179.5
Slovakia	33.2	10.9	6.4	4.1	23.6	6.7	0.2	85.1
Ukraine	12.9	0.8	10.6	5.0	4.9	3.7	5.4	43.3
Total	246.3	126.1	147.4	181.8	180.6	100.7	110.9	1,093.8

Source: Lemer, Jeremy, Steven Bernard, and Helen Warrell, Eastern Exposure, Financial Times, February 25, 2009.

Since the fall of 2008, the European Union has moved to address the long-term needs of the financial system. As a key component of this approach, the EU commissioned a group within the EU to assess the weaknesses of the existing EU financial architecture. It also charged this group with developing proposals that could help guide the EU in fashioning a system that would provide early warning of areas of financial weakness and chart a way forward in erecting a stronger financial system. As part of this way forward, the European Union issued two reports in the first quarter of 2009 that address the issue of supervision of financial markets. The first report[9], issued on February 25, 2009 and commissioned by the European Union, was prepared by a high-level group on financial supervision headed by former IMF Managing Director and ex- Bank of France Governor Jacques de Larosiere and is known as the de Larosiere Report. The second report[10] was published by the European

Commission to chart the course ahead for the members of the EU to reform the international financial governance system.

The de Larosiere Report recommends that the EU create a new macro-prudential level of supervision called the European Systemic Risk Council (ESRC) chaired by the President of the European Central Bank. A driving force behind creating the ESRC is that it would bring together the central banks of all of the EU members with a clear mandate to preserve financial stability by collectively forming judgments and making recommendations on macro-prudential policy. The ESRC would also gather information on all macro-prudential risks in the EU, decide on macro- prudential policy, provide early risk warning to EU supervisors, compare observations on macroeconomic and prudential developments, and give direction on the aforementioned issues.

Next, the Report recommends that the EU create a new European System of Financial Supervision (ESFS) to transform a group of EU committees known as L3 Committees[11] into EU Authorities. The three L3 Committees are: the Committee of European Securities Regulators (CESR); the Committee of European Banking Supervisors (CEBS); and the Committee of European Insurance and Occupational Pensions Supervisors (CEIOPS). The ESFS would maintain the decentralized structure that characterizes the current system of national supervisors, while the ESFS would coordinate the actions of the national authorities to maintain common high level supervisory standards, guarantee strong cooperation with other supervisors, and guarantee that the interests of the host supervisors are properly safeguarded.

"Driving European Recovery," issued by the European Commission, presents a slightly different approach to financial supervision and recovery than that proposed by the de Larosiere group, although it accepts many of the recommendations offered by the group. The recommendations in the report were intended to complement the economic stimulus measures that were adopted by the EU on November 27, 2008 under the $256 billion Economic Recovery Plan[12] that funds cross- border projects, including investments in clean energy and upgraded telecommunications infrastructure. The plan is meant to ensure that, "all relevant actors and all types of financial investments are subject to appropriate regulation and oversight." In particular, the EC plan notes that nation-based financial supervisory models are lagging behind the market reality of a large number of financial institutions that operate across national borders.

The current financial and economic crises, however, have exposed deep philosophical differences among EU members over the most effective policy course to pursue to address these two crises. EU members have addressed the financial crisis independently and in concert through the EU organization, reflecting the dual nature of the EU system. Unlike the United States, where the Federal government can implement policies that are applied systematically across all 50 States, EU-wide actions reflect compromise among national authorities. As a result, the national authorities exercise considerable freedom in implementing EU Directives and in charting their own response to the crisis. For instance, EU members agreed to support an EU-wide fiscal stimulus to counter the economic downturn. The worsening economic conditions in Europe, however, have not been felt evenly across all EU members, and their response has exposed differences in economic philosophies that have blunted a coordinated approach. EU members also have responded differently to helping banks reduce their exposure to so-called toxic loans, because in the current environment their market value cannot be determined. The efforts by some EU members to address this issue has pushed the EU to consider an EU-wide approach.

Within the EU, however, integration of the financial services sector across borders has been uneven, with integration progressing faster in the money, bond, and equity markets, and slowest in the banking sector where many of the policy changes likely will be focused. According to the European Central Bank,[13] retail banking services remain segmented along national lines as a result of differences in national tax laws, costs of national registration and compliance, and cultural preferences. Nevertheless, cross-border mergers and acquisitions within Europe have played an important role in internationalizing banking groups, which has led to significant cross- border banking activity. Integration within the banking sector in Europe also has increased since the European Community adopted the euro as the EU's single currency.

The EU response to the two crises has been complicated further by a number of factors, including the need to mesh new proposals with such existing EU Directives as the Stability and Growth Pact[14], the Lisbon Principles[15], and the Financial Services Action Plan.[16] The EU structure gives the individual members considerable latitude to formulate their own policies in response to crises.

In some cases, this has meant that the EU has had to adopt policies that have been implemented by some of its members to prevent a sort of EU-wide competition. For instance, EU members were pressed to support a broad set of measures to increase the guarantees on bank accounts for depositors in response to actions by Ireland, Greece, and Germany. Some EU members are also considering procedures to deal with the bad loans of banks within their jurisdictions, which has pushed the EU as a whole to follow suit and consider the best approach to deal with the toxic loans of EU banks. This and other issues have exposed sharp differences among the EU members over the best approach to deal with financial market reforms and economic stimulus measures. These differences may well become more pronounced as multilateral discussions shift from addressing the general goal of containing the financial crisis to the more contentious issues of specific market reforms, regulations, and supervision.

Economic Performance

Estimates developed by the International Monetary Fund in January 2009 provide a rough indicator of the impact the financial crisis and an economic recession are having on the performance of major advanced countries. Economic growth in Europe is expected to slow by nearly 2% in 2009 to post a 0.2% drop in the rate of economic growth, while the threat of inflation is expected to lessen, as indicated in **Table 2**. Economic growth, as represented by gross domestic product (GDP), is expected to register a negative 1.6% rate for the United States in 2009, while the euro area countries could experience a combined negative rate of 2.0%, down from a projected rate of growth of 1.2% in 2008. The sharp drop in the prices of oil and other commodities in the later part of 2008 may have helped improve the rate of economic growth, but the length and depth of the economic downturn likely well mean that the IMF projections prove to be too optimistic when the final data for 2009 are known. Indeed, in mid-February, the European Union announced that the rate of economic growth in the EU in the fourth quarter of 2008 had slowed to an annual rate of negative 6%.[17]

THE FINANCIAL CRISIS AND THE EUROPEAN UNION

The cause and effects of the current financial crisis likely will be debated for years to come. This report does not attempt to provide a complete explanation of the causes of the financial crisis, since other CRS Reports address these issues.[18] While different individuals and organizations view the crisis from different perspectives, one way to view the crisis is as a series of policy events proceeding through four periods where the policy responses differed.[19] The periods are not necessarily discretely identifiable, because they overlap with other periods, or the policy responses have been repeated as the financial crisis has persisted. This has been especially true as the financial crisis has deepened over time and as the economic downturn and the financial crisis have become reinforcing events, compounding efforts to resolve either crisis.

Table 2. Projections of Economic Growth in Various Countries and Areas (real GDP growth, in percent change)

	2007	2008	2009	2010
Actual		Projected		
World	5.2	3.4	0.5	3.0
United States	2.0	1.1	−1.6	1.6
Advanced Economies	2.7	1.0	−2.0	1.1
Emerging Economies	8.3	6.3	3.3	5.0
European Union	3.1	1.3	−1.8	0.5
Euro Area	2.6	1.0	-2.0	0.2
France	2.2	0.8	-1.9	0.7
Germany	2.5	1.3	-2.5	0.1
Italy	1.5	-0.6	-2.1	-0.1
Spain	2.4	-0.3	-2.6	0.6
United Kingdom	3.0	0.7	-2.8	0.2
Non-EU advanced	4.6	1.9	-2.4	2.2
Japan	2.4	-0.3	-2.6	0.6
Canada	2.7	0.6	-1.2	1.6

Source: *World Economic Outlook, Update*, the International Monetary Fund, January 2009.

The first phase of the crisis represents the early build-up to the crisis in which policymakers responded in an *ad hoc* manner to assist individually troubled banks and financial institutions. In the second phase, national governments, primarily through central banks, moved to address issues of liquidity that arose from wide-spread concerns over the viability of the financial system, rather than the more narrow concerns of individual institutions. In the third phase, government finance ministries adopted policies to address issues of solvency as banks and other financial firms attempted to deleverage their positions by reducing their holdings of troubled assets and as credit markets essentially shut down. In the fourth phase, governments, through finance ministries and legislative bodies, shifted to address growing concerns over the economic downturn that has worsened the financial crisis.

According to reports by the International Monetary Fund (IMF) and the European Central Bank (ECB), many of the factors that led to the financial crisis in the United States created a similar crisis in Europe.[20] Essentially low interest rates and an expansion of financial and investment opportunities that arose from aggressive credit expansion, growing complexity in mortgage securitization, and loosening in underwriting standards combined with expanded linkages among national financial centers to spur a broad expansion in credit and economic growth. This rapid rate of growth pushed up the values of equities, commodities, and real estate. Over time, the combination of higher commodity prices and rising housing costs pinched consumers' budgets, and they began reducing their expenditures. One consequence of this drop in consumer spending was a slowdown in economic activity and, eventually, a contraction in the prices of housing. In turn, the decline in the prices of housing led to a large-scale downgrade in the ratings of subprime mortgage-backed securities and the closing of a number of hedge funds with subprime exposure. Concerns over the pricing of risk in the market for subprime mortgage-backed securities spread to other financial markets, including to structured securities more generally and the interbank money market. Problems spread quickly throughout the financial sector to include financial guarantors as the markets turned increasingly dysfunctional over fears of under valued assets.

PHASE I – BUILD-UP

The first phase of the financial crisis is identified with a loss of confidence in credit markets that was associated with a downturn in the U.S. housing market caused primarily by rising defaults in subprime mortgages. In this stage, EU governments generally responded on a case-by-case basis, without a role for the broader Community. A sharp downturn in mortgage markets generally would be expected to have a negative impact on parts of the economy, but the current financial crisis quickly evolved into a more general liquidity crisis that spread well beyond the sub-prime mortgage market. Initially, only highly leveraged banks, investment firms, and other financial services providers seemed to be affected by the credit problems. During this phase in the United States, the Federal Deposit Insurance Corporation took control of IndyMac Bank.

Table 3. Elements of Banking System Rescue Plans in European Countries

Country	Expansion of retail deposit insurance	Guarantee of wholesale liabilities — New debt	Guarantee of wholesale liabilities — Existing debt	Capital injections	Asset purchases
Austria	X	X		X	
Belgium	X	X			
Denmark	X	X	X		
Finland	X				
France		X		X	
Germany	X	X		X	X
Greece	X	X		X	
Ireland	X	X	X		
Italy		X			
Netherlands	X	X			
Norway					X
Portugal	X	X			
Spain	X	X		X	X
Sweden	X	X		X	
Switzerland				X	X
United Kingdom	X	X		X	X

Source: Fender, Ingo, and Jacob Gyntelberg, Overview: global financial Crisis Spurs Unprecedented Policy Actions, *Quarterly Review*, Bank for International Settlements, December 2008, p. 11.

The financial crisis that began in the United States as a result of a downturn in residential property values quickly spread to European banks through effects felt in the market for asset-backed commercial paper (ABCP).[21] European banks were either directly holding the securities or they were holding them indirectly through conduits and structured investment vehicles with similar holdings. As the ABCP market collapsed, banks holding such securities were forced to step in with additional funding, which squeezed liquidity in the global financial market through the interbank market. Over time, banks and other financial firms found that it was impossible to price the value of assets that were being used to back commercial paper. During this phase, the British government nationalized housing lender Northern Rock and Bradford & Bingley, a mortgage lender. Belgium, France, and Luxembourg governments and shareholders provided capital to Dexia, the world's largest lender to municipalities, and Belgian, Dutch, and Luxembourg governments injected $16.4 billion into banking and insurance company Fortis to head off the first major bank crisis in the Euro area.

PHASE II – LIQUIDITY ISSUES

In the second phase, policy shifted from an ad hoc focus on the fate of individual firms to concerns over troubled markets as central banks intervened to lower interest rates, to provide liquidity, and to provide foreign currency. In the United States, as generally is the case in most countries, the Federal Reserve, or the central bank, holds a monopoly over the conduct of monetary policy, mainly as a means of keeping such policy-making independent from political pressure. Normally, it is not the role of the central bank to be the main provider of liquidity, but that role falls to the central banks as lenders of last resort during periods of financial crisis. In addition, central banks generally share regulatory and supervisory responsibilities, including providing assistance to individual firms or helping banks deleverage, with a number of different agencies that are more directly accountable to elected officials and are subject to change.

During this phase, governments attempted to stabilize the financial markets by expanding insurance on guarantees for depositors and, in some cases, guarantees for banks. Central banks also engaged in direct injections of capital to support the balance sheets of banks and removed some distressed assets from banks by acquiring the assets. Efforts to acquire distressed assets from the banks, however, raised questions concerning the value of the assets, since, in most cases, the value of the assets had fallen below the value indicated on the balance sheets of the banks. The Bank for International Settlements (BIS) indicates that governments in Europe varied their responses to the financial crisis, as indicated in **Table 3**. In addition, the BIS indicates that there are considerable differences in the design and implementation of the rescue efforts and in the way foreign depositors are treated in the case of a bank failure.

In this phase, Iceland was especially hard hit by the financial crisis, with major Icelandic banks completely shutting down for a period of time.[22] On November 19, 2008, Iceland and the International Monetary Fund (IMF) finalized an agreement on an economic stabilization program supported by a $2.1 billion two-year standby arrangement from the IMF.[23] Following the IMF decision, Denmark, Finland, Norway, and Sweden agreed to provide an additional $2.5 billion. On January 26, 2009, public protests against the Icelandic government's handling of the crisis and the economy caused Iceland's Prime Minister Haarde to resign and the coalition government to fall.

Central Bank Operations

During this phase, U.S. mortgage markets continued to deteriorate, prompting the U.S. Treasury and Federal Reserve to engineer the acquisition of Bear Stearns by JPMorgan Chase and to announce that it was taking over the Federal National Mortgage Association (Fannie Mae) and the Federal Home Loan Mortgage Corporation (Freddie Mac). Soon after this takeover, Lehman Brothers filed for bankruptcy, which led to a more wide-spread crisis of confidence, and which, in turn, led credit markets to freeze up and led to a lack of liquidity. Given Lehman's far-reaching exposure in the financial markets, its collapse likely would have had a negative impact on the financial markets under normal circumstances, but the impact was magnified by underlying weaknesses in the markets that had been building over time. In particular, Lehman was heavily involved in the $57 trillion credit default swap (CDS)[24] market. Lehman's bankruptcy triggered clauses in CDS contracts that referenced Lehman, and it terminated contracts that Lehman had entered into as a counterparty.[25] Lehman also originated commercial paper and other forms of short term debt that a number of European banks held through Lehman's global presence. As investors scrambled to redeem commercial paper, the Federal Reserve stepped in to the money markets and purchased commercial paper and other short term money market securities. Particularly hard hit by the Lehman bankruptcy was AIG (American International Group), which had been closely tied to the CDSs offered by Lehman. The Federal Reserve arranged for a $85 billion credit facility in exchange for an 80% equity stake in AIG.

Various governments, through their central banks, injected capital directly into banks and other financial firms during this phase to keep firms from failing and to arrange mergers by providing liquidity. The British government arranged for Halifax Bank of Scotland (HBOS) to be acquired by the Lloyds Banking Group. In the United States, the Office of Thrift of Supervision seized Washington Mutual Bank from Washington Mutual, Inc. and arranged for its sale to JPMorgan Chase. The Federal Reserve also approved the transformation of Goldman Sachs and Morgan Stanley into bank holding companies.

According to a paper prepared by staff at the International Monetary Fund (IMF),[26] one of the key issues facing central banks during the crisis has been distinguishing between troubled markets and troubled institutions. Troubled institutions can be dealt with on a case-by-case basis, as was done in the initial stages of the financial crisis. Troubled markets, however, require a more coordinated approach since the effects can span a range of countries and financial markets. The authors also concluded that central banks were able to respond quickly to the financial crisis as a result of various aspects of their operational framework that allowed them to respond without fundamentally changing their basic monetary policy. While it is important for central banks to be flexible when responding to a crisis, the study emphasized, central banks, "cannot come to be seen as the market maker of last resort in all markets nor the lender of last resort for all institutions." The authors concluded that central bank policies should strike a balance between supporting the financial system during times of crisis and setting in motion the seeds of future crises. Also, the study indicated that certain types of central bank mechanisms proved to be more effective in providing liquidity and in coping with significant turbulence in the financial markets.

The European Central Bank provided large quantities of reserves through routine short-term open-market operations and through longer-term open market operations. Unlike the Federal Reserve, which normally conducts open market operations with a small set of primary dealers against a narrow range of highly liquid collateral, the ECB routinely conducts open market operations with a wide range of counterparties against a broad range of collateral. The ECB extended this strategy during this phase of the financial crisis with a longer term refinancing operation.[27] This greater flexibility, compared with the Federal Reserve, reportedly made it possible for the ECB to provide liquidity within its existing framework without resorting to extraordinary measures.[28] During this phase, the UK's Financial Services Authority arranged for the sale of a large part of Bradford & Bingley to the Spanish bank Grupo Santander, while Fortis a banking and insurance company received a capital injection from the Belgian, Dutch, and Luxembourg governments.

During this phase, the British Government announced a $850 billion multi-part plan to rescue its banking sector from the financial crisis, known as the Stability and Reconstruction Plan. The key feature of the plan, as promoted by British Prime Minister Gordon Brown, has the central government acquiring preferred shares in distressed banks for a specified amount of time, rather than acquiring the non-performing loans of the banks. The announcement of the Plan followed a day when British banks lost more than $25 billion on the London Stock Exchange. The biggest loser was the Royal Bank of Scotland, whose shares fell 39%, representing $15 billion, of lost value. In the downturn, other British banks lost substantial amounts of their value, including the Halifax Bank of Scotland which was in the process of being acquired by Lloyds TSB. The British plan is comprised of four parts:

- First was a coordinated cut in key interest rates of 50 basis points, or one-half of one percent (0.5) with the Bank of England, the Federal Reserve, and the European Central Bank all participating.
- Second was an announcement of an investment facility of $87 billion implemented in two stages to acquire the Tier 1 capital, or preferred stock, in "eligible" banks and building societies (financial institutions that specialize on mortgage financing) in order to recapitalize the firms. Under the financial plan, eight British banks – Abbey, RBS, Barclays, Hallifax Bank of Scotland, HSBC (Hong Kong and Shanghai Banking Corporation), Lloyds TSB, Standard Chartered, and Nationwide Building Society – signed up to participate in the recapitalization effort.
- Third, the British Government agreed to make available to those institutions participating in the recapitalization scheme up to $436 billion in guarantees on new short- and medium-term debt to assist in refinancing maturing funding obligations as they fall due for terms up to three years.
- Fourth, the British Government announced that it would make available $352 billion through the Special Liquidity Scheme[29] to improve liquidity in the banking industry.[30]

In addition to this four-part plan, the Bank of England announced that it had developed three new proposals for its money market operations. First, was the establishment of Operational Standing Facilities that are aimed at addressing technical problems and imbalances in the operation of money markets and payments facilities, although they did not provide financial support. Second, the establishment of a Discount Window Facility which allows banks to borrow government bonds or, at the Bank's discretion, cash, against a wide range of eligible collateral to provide liquidity insurance to commercial banks in stress. Third, a permanent open market for long-tem repurchase agreements (securities sold for cash with an agreement to repurchase the securities at a specified time) against broader classes of collateral to offer banks additional tools for managing their liquidity.[31] The plan was quickly implemented with the UK government taking a controlling interest in the Royal Bank of Scotland (RBS) and Hallifax Bank of Scotland (HBOS).

At the euro area summit on October 12, 2008, the euro area countries, along with the United Kingdom, urged all European governments to adopt a common set of principles to address the financial crisis.[32] The measures the nations supported were largely in line with those that had been proposed by the United Kingdom and included:

- Recapitalization: governments promised to provide funds to banks that might be struggling to raise capital and pledged to pursue wide-ranging restructuring of the leadership of those banks that are turning to the government for capital.
- State ownership: governments indicated that they will buy shares in the banks that are seeking recapitalization.
- Government debt guarantees: guarantees offered for any new debts, including inter-bank loans, issued by the banks in the euro zone area.
- Improved regulations: the governments agreed to encourage regulations to permit assets to be valued on their risk of default, instead of their current market price.

In addition to these measures, EU leaders agreed on October 16, 2008, to set up a crisis unit and they agreed to a monthly meeting to improve financial oversight.[33] Jose Manuel Barroso, President of the European Commission, urged EU members to develop a "fully integrated solution" to address the global financial crisis, consistent with France's support for a strong international organization to oversee the financial markets. The EU members expressed their support for the current approach within the EU, which makes each EU member responsible for developing and implementing its own national regulations regarding supervision over financial institutions. The European Council stressed the need to strengthen the supervision of the European financial sector. As a result, the EU statement urged the EU members to develop a "coordinated supervision system at the European level."[34] This approach likely will be tested as a result of failed talks with the credit derivatives industry in Europe. In early January 2009, an EUsponsored working group reported that it had failed to get a commitment from the credit derivatives industry to use a central clearing house for credit default swaps. As an alternative, the European Commission reportedly is considering adopting a set of rules for EU members that would require banks and other users of the CDS markets to use a central clearing house within the EU as a way of reducing risk.[35]

Interest Rates

On October 8, 2008, central banks in the United States, the Eurozone, the United Kingdom, Canada, Sweden, and Switzerland staged a coordinated cut in interest rates to improve liquidity, and they announced that they had a plan of action to address the ever-widening financial crisis.[36] Soon after, the U.S. Treasury, in coordination with the Federal Reserve, announced its Capital Purchase Program as part of its Troubled Asset Relief Program and arranged for an injection of capital in exchange for equity shares into eight major U.S. banks.[37] On October 29, 2008, the U.S. Federal Reserve cut key interest rates by half a percentage point, a move that was matched by China and Norway.[38] In response to these cuts, on November 6, 2008, the Bank of England cut its key interest rates by 1.5 percent points to 3%. The cut was three times larger than any seen since the central bank's monetary policy committee was established in 1997.[39] At the same time, the European Central Bank (ECB), which sets interest rates for the 16 members of the Eurozone, cut its interest rates by half a percentage point to 3.25%.[40] The Czech Central Bank also cut its rates by a larger than expected three-quarters of a percentage point, while the Swiss National Bank lowered its rates by one-half of a percentage point. The cut in rates came as the IMF published an emergency update of its economic forecasts, predicting that the economies of the developed countries would shrink by 0.3% in 2009, down from a projection released in October that growth among the most developed economies would increase by 0.5%.

Currency Swap Facilities

In addition to reducing interest rates and providing liquidity by injecting capital directly into banks, the Federal Reserve and other central banks in Europe and elsewhere expanded short-term bilateral currency swap facilities by $180 billion to compensate for a dollar liquidity crisis. The dollar is used widely in international trade transactions and as a reserve currency by other central banks. The dollar is also used by many financial institutions outside the United States that have substantially increased their dollar investments, including loans to nonbanks and purchases of asset-backed securities issued by U.S. firms. Most financial institutions outside the United States have relied on interbank and other wholesale markets to obtain dollars. As credit markets seized up, however, these institutions found they did not have access to short-term dollar financing. European banks, in particular, had difficulties obtaining US dollar funding. Preceding the financial crisis, European banks had vastly expanded their accumulation of dollars in the interbank market and from official monetary authorities that had acquired dollar-denominated assets. In essence, European banks borrowed dollars short term in the interbank market in order to finance a rapid growth in investments in dollar-denominated assets with varying maturities in assets held by non-banks, such as asset-backed commercial paper, which left European banks with large short-term US dollar funding requirements. Such constant refinancing contributed to the squeeze in liquidity and to problems in obtaining dollars in the foreign exchange market and in cross-country currency swap markets.[41]

The principal tool the Federal Reserve and the European Central Bank used to counter the currency shortage is a temporary currency swap, which allows central banks to borrow currency from each other in order to relend the currencies to banks in their jurisdictions. Typically, inter- central bank foreign exchange swap arrangements are used to support foreign exchange market intervention, rather than to alleviate shortages of foreign exchange in the short-term funding market. Prior to September 2008, the Federal Reserve had established inter-central bank currency swap lines with the Swiss National Bank and with the European Central Bank to deliver U.S. dollar funds, complimenting the Federal Reserve's Term Auction Facility. Between September 2008 and November 2008, the Federal Reserve established such arrangements with more than a dozen other central banks.[42]

In addition to shortages of dollars, there have also been shortages of euros and Swiss francs. During the period when the European Central Bank was concluding swap arrangements with the Federal Reserve, it was also establishing currency swaps with the Czech central bank, the National Bank of Denmark, and the National Bank of Poland. Central banks in Europe responded to the currency shortage by providing currency from their own foreign exchange reserves and by borrowing from other central banks, principally from the central bank that issued the currency.

Depositor Guarantees

Ireland, Greece, and Germany also increased their guarantees to deposit holders to improve liquidity in the financial system, a move that was adopted by the EU as a whole to curtail a form of regulatory competition for depositors. The International Monetary Fund also approved a short-term liquidity facility to assist banks facing liquidity problems. The G-7[43] group of countries met to discuss a coordinated approach to the crisis,[44] followed by the Euro area summit, at which the Euro area countries urged all European governments to help recapitalize banks, to have governments buy shares in banks, if needed, to guarantee the debt of banks, and to improve bank regulations.[45]

On December 4, 2008, European central banks initiated another round of cuts in interest rates. The ECB cut its key rate by three-quarters of a percentage point to 2.5%, representing the largest one-day rate move in the bank's 10-year history. In turn, the Bank of England cut its key rate by a full percentage point to 2%. Sweden's central bank also cut interest rates by 1.75 percentage points to 2%, the largest single cut in rates in 16 years.[46] On January 8, 2009, the Bank of England reduced its Official Bank Rate by 0.5 percentage points to 1.5%.[47] In addition, on February 5, 2009, the Bank of England announced an additional cut in its official bank rate by 0.5% to 1.0% to stimulate economic growth.[48] On January 15, 2009, the ECB President Jean-Claude Trichet announced that the bank had cut its rates by 0.5% to 2.0% as a result of lower inflationary pressures and weakening economic prospects due to reduced exports and lower domestic demand within the EU countries.[49] In summing up, Trichet indicated that the reasoning behind the ECB's decision was based on a number of factors:

> This takes into account the latest economic data releases and survey information, which add clear further evidence to the assessment that the euro area is experiencing a significant slowdown, largely related to the effects of the intensification and broadening of the financial turmoil. Both global demand and euro area demand are likely to be dampened for a protracted period. All in all, the level of uncertainty remains exceptionally high.[50]

PHASE III – SOLVENCY AND DELEVERAGING

In the third phase, the lack of confidence in credit markets and a lack of liquidity also sparked concerns over the adequacy of capital provisions of financial institutions and concerns over the solvency of banks and other financial firms. During this phase, financial firms attempted to deleverage by reducing the amount of troubled assets they held on their balance sheets. At the same time, the stocks of most financial firms in the United States and in Europe dropped markedly, and the value of their assets deteriorated, which weakened the financial position of an even larger number of firms. In this phase, intervention by central banks continued, but national governments also began to intervene, typically through their respective Treasury departments, to take control of insolvent banks or otherwise to provide financial assistance. The U.S. Congress passed the Troubled Assets Relief Program as part of the Emergency Economic Stabilization Act (P.L. 110-343) initially intended to acquire up to $700 billion in troubled mortgage-related securities.[51] As the financial crisis persisted, U.S. Treasury Secretary Geithner announced on February 9, 2009, that the Financial Stability Plan that was being prepared at that time by the Treasury Department provided a "full arsenal of financial tools and the resources commensurate" to stress test banks; to provide for a public-private investment fund; to provide funds for consumer and business lending; and to ensure greater transparency, accountability, and monitoring of banks.[52]

The "European Framework for Action"

On October 29, 2008, the European Commission released its "European Framework for Action" as a way to coordinate the actions of the 27 members of the European Union in addressing the financial crisis.[53] On November 16, 2008, the Commission announced a more detailed plan that brings together short-term goals to address the current economic downturn with the longer-term goals on growth and jobs that are integral to the Lisbon Strategy for Growth and Jobs that was adopted by the EU in 2000 and recast in 2005. The short-term plan focuses on a three-part approach to an overall EU recovery action plan/framework. The three parts to the EU framework are: 1) a new financial market architecture at the EU-level; 2) dealing with the impact on the real economy; and 3) a global response to the financial crisis.

- **A new financial market architecture at the EU level.** The basis of this architecture involves implementing measures that EU members have announced as well as providing for: 1) continued support for the financial system from the European Central Bank and other central banks; 2) rapid and consistent implementation on the bank rescue plan that has been established by the member states; and 3) decisive measures that are designed to contain the crisis from spreading to all of the member states. As the financial system is stabilized, the next step is to restructure the banking sector and to return banks to the private sector. Proposals include: deposit guarantees and capital requirements; regulation and accounting standards; credit rating agencies, executive pay; capital market supervision, and risk management.

- **Dealing with the impact on the real economy.** The policy instruments that can be employed to address the expected rise in unemployment and decline in economic growth are in the hands of the member states. Nevertheless, the EU can assist by adding short-term actions to its structural reform agenda, while investing in the future through: 1) increasing investment in R&D innovation and education; 2) promoting "flexicurity"[54] to protect and equip people rather than specific jobs; 3) freeing up businesses to build markets at home and internationally; and 4) enhancing competitiveness by promoting green technology, and overcoming energy security constraints and achieving environmental goals. In addition, the Commission will explore a wide range of ways in which EU members can increase their rate of economic growth.

- The impact of the financial crisis on the real economies of the EU members likely will require adjustments in the fiscal and monetary policies of the EU members. The Stability and Growth Pact[55] of the EU members should serve as the blueprint for members facing higher than expected levels of fiscal or monetary stimulus so that such policies should be accompanied by structural reforms. Such reforms should aim to sustain domestic demand in the short-run, ease transitions within and into the labor market, and increase potential growth by directing investment into areas that will sustain employment and advance productivity. Reforms in the finance sector should focus on enhancing the competitive position of the European industry and finance the needs of small and medium-sized firms. The Commission will also attempt to counter an expected increase in unemployment by using funds provided under the European Social Fund[56] to reintroduce unemployed workers back into the work force.

- **A global response to the financial crisis.** The crisis has raised questions concerning global governance that are relative to the financial sector and to the need to maintain open trade markets. The EU intended to use the November 15, 2008 multi-nation economic summit In Washington D.C. to promote a series of measures to reform the global financial architecture. The Commission argued that the measures should include: 1) strengthening international regulatory standards; 2) strengthening international coordination among financial supervisors; 3) strengthening measures to monitor and coordinate macroeconomic policies; and 4) developing the capacity to address a financial crisis at the national regional and multilateral levels. Also, a financial architecture plan should include three key principles: 1) efficiency; 2) transparency and accountability; and 3) inclusion of representation from key emerging economies.

In concert with the European Framework for action, several European countries, including Germany, France, Italy, Austria, Netherlands, Portugal, Spain, and Norway announced plans to recapitalize banks and to provide government debt guarantees. European leaders agreed to increase the role of the IMF in preventing a future financial crisis, however, they could not agree on precisely what that role should be.[57] As a consequence, the leaders set a 100-day deadline to draw up reforms for the international financial system and asked the Bank for International Settlements (BIS) to develop a set of guidelines to ensure that banks hold enough capital to reduce the risks of a similar financial crisis.

On January 7, 2009, the BIS responded to the request by the G20 by publishing a first draft of its proposed guidelines[58] for "stress testing banks," or assessing the impact of various large shocks on the ability of banks to absorb losses. Stress testing is a risk management tool that is used by banks to assess the financial position of a bank under a severe but plausible scenario to absorb the impact of unexpected risks on the bank's capital position, which is comprised of common stock and retained earnings. Banks do not loan out their capital directly to borrowers, but use it as a cushion to help them absorb losses from loans and other banking activities. Currently, banks are required to engage in periodic stress testing as a risk management tool. The BIS guidelines provide a set of recommendations for bank supervisors as they review the conduct of stress tests within their banks in order to overcome shortcomings in the present system that failed to assess such risks as: the behavior of complex structured products; risks in relation to hedging strategies; pipeline or securitization risk; contingent risk; and funding liquidity risk.

"Bad Banks"

The United Kingdom, the Netherlands, Germany, and the European Central Bank are considering proposals to split off the bad assets of banks into a separate "bad bank" to prevent more banks from failing as did Sweden in the 1990s and Switzerland in 2008. The economic downturn is continuing to erode the value of the assets that banks are holding as capital, which is causing banks to curtail their lending and, in a growing number of cases, threatening the viability of the bank. The United Kingdom created such a bank when it took over Bradford & Bingley by selling off the healthy portion of the bank and holding "bad" assets. A hurdle that faces a bank with bad assets is that when the bank participates in such a bad asset program they are forced to lower the value they assign to their bad assets before they can move them to a bad bank, which further dilutes the value of the remaining shares of the bank and compounds the efforts by the bank to raise capital.[59]

Germany is considering a plan that would shift bad assets from banks into special-purpose securities with government guarantees. Officials are also considering providing more generous accounting rules that would protect assets that experience a down grade in their value from having a negative impact on the value of the capital a bank uses to support its core business. In response to actions by Germany and the United Kingdom, the European Central Bank is drawing up guidelines for European governments that are considering establishing "bad" banks to forestall a competitive movement by EU governments. The ECB is also considering guidelines for some governments that are developing plans to guarantee the bad assets that remain on the books of banks to head off a move to gain a competitive advantage for some banks.[60]

PHASE IV – FISCAL INTERVENTION

In the fourth phase, as the problems in credit markets persisted, the financial crisis spread to those activities in the real economy that are highly reliant on credit markets, and it reinforced concerns over the adequacy of capital provisions. Furthermore, the slowdown in economic growth weakened the capital position of financial institutions so that the financial crisis and the economic downturn have become negatively reinforcing. Governments have responded in this phase of the crisis by adopting macroeconomic stimulus measures to blunt the effects of the economic recession. In February 2008, Congress passed P.L. 110-185, the Economic Stimulus Act of 2008 to provide rebates to individuals on their income taxes in order to provide a fiscal boost to the U.S. economy.[61] Then in July 2008, Congress adopted, and President Bush signed, P.L. 110-289, the Housing and Economic Recovery Act of 2008 to provide an additional fiscal stimulus to the U.S. economy. In February 2009, as the U.S. economy continued to post large monthly losses in jobs, Congress adopted, and President Obama signed, a compromise measure of H.R. 1, the American Recovery and Reinvestment Act of 2009 to provide an additional fiscal stimulus to the U.S. economy. The British, French, and German governments also announced fiscal stimulus packages. Various central banks announced additional cuts in key interest rates as another effort to stimulate economic growth. On March 5, 2009, the European Central Bank and the Bank of England announced a cut in key interest rates by 0.5% to 1.5% and 0.5%, respectively, approaching the Federal Reserve rate of 0.25%. In addition, the Bank of England announced a quantitative easing in monetary policy, or increasing the money supply, by $150 billion over three months to stimulate economic growth.[62]

European Economic Recovery Plan

On November 27, 2008, the European Commission proposed a $256 billion Economic Recovery Plan[63] that would fund cross-border projects, including investments in clean energy and upgraded telecommunications infrastructure. In all, the European Economic Recovery Plan is comprised of two parts. First, each EU member is asked to contribute an amount equivalent to 1.5% of their GDP to boost consumer demand. Second, members are tasked to invest in energy efficient equipment to create jobs and save energy, invest in

The Financial Crisis: Impact on and Response by the European Union

environmentally clean technologies to convert such sectors as construction and automobiles to low-carbon sectors, and to invest in infrastructure and communications. The members of the European Council approved the plan in a meeting on December 12, 2008. As **Table 4** indicates, most European countries have announced some form of an economic stimulus package.

Table 4. Announced and Planned or Proposed Stimulus Packages

Date Announced	Country	$ in billions	Status, Package Contents
12-Dec-08	European Union	256.00	Fund cross-border projects including clean energy and upgraded telecommunications architecture. Each EU member to contribute an amount equivalent to 1.5% of GDP to boost consumer spending. Members asked to boost spending in energy efficient equipment and clean
13-Jan-09	Germany	65.00	Infrastructure, tax cuts, child bonus, increase in some social benefits, $3,250 incentive for trading in cars more than nine years old for a new or slightly used car.
24-Nov-08	United Kingdom	29.60	Proposed plan includes a 2.5% cut in the value added tax for 13 months, a postponement of corporate tax increases, government guarantees for loans to small and midsize businesses, spending on public works, including public housing and energy efficiency. Plan includes an increase in income taxes on those making more than $225,000 and increase National Insurance contribution for all but the lowest income workers.
5-Nov-08	France	33.00	Public sector investments (road and rail construction, refurbishment and improving ports and river infrastructure, building and renovating universities, research centers, prisons, courts, and monuments) and loans for carmakers. Does not include the previously planned $15 billion in credits and tax breaks on investments by companies in 2009.

Table 4. (Continued)

Date Announced	Country	$ in billions	Status, Package Contents
16-Nov-08	Italy	52.00	Awaiting final parliamentary approval. Three year program. Measures to spur consumer credit, provide loans to companies, and rebuild infrastructure. February 6, announced a $2.56 billion stimulus package that was part of the three-year program that includes payments of up to $1,950 for trading in an old car for a new, less polluting one and 20% tax deductions for purchases of appliances and furniture.
22-Nov-08	Netherlands	7.50	Tax deduction to companies that make large investments, funds to companies that hire temporary workers, and creation of a program to find jobs for the unemployed.
11-Dec-08	Belgium	2.60	Increase in unemployment benefits, lowering of the value added tax on construction, abolishing taxes on energy, energy checks for families, faste payments of invoices by the government, faster government investment Irailroads and buildings, and lowering of employer's fiscal contributions.
27-Nov-08	Spain	14.30	Public works, help for automobile industry, environmental projects, research and development, restoring residential and military housing, and funds to support the sick.
14-Jan-09	Portugal	2.89	Funds to be provided to medium and small-sized businesses, money for infrastructure, particularly schools, and investment in technological improvement.
20-Nov-08	Israel	5.40	Public works to include desalination plants, doubling railway routes, adding R&D funding, increasing export credits, cutting assorted taxes, and aid packages for employers to hire new workers.

Table 4. (Continued)

Date Announced	Country	$ in billions	Status, Package Contents
21-Dec-08	Switzerland	0.59	Public works spending on flood defense, natural disaster and energy efficiency projects.
5-Dec-08	Sweden	2.70	Public infrastructure and investment in human capital, including job training, vocational workshops, and workplace restructuring.; extension of social benefits to part-time workers.
26-Jan-09	Norway	2.88	Investment in construction, infrastructure, and renovation of state-owned buildings, tax breaks for companies.

Source: Various news articles.
Notes: Amounts are in U.S. dollars. Currency conversions to U.S. dollars were done in the news articles or by using current exchange rates.

As part of the EC plan, budget rules imposed by the Stability and Growth Pact would be loosened to allow EU members to adopt economic stimulus plans to shore up their declining economic growth rates. The plan is intended to mesh with the goals and objectives outlined in the Lisbon Strategy to improve the rate of economic growth among EU members. This plan also proposes official support measures to increase the rate of employment and to focus investments on such high technology sectors as telecommunications and environmentally safe technologies. In addition to the proposed macroeconomic stimulus plan, various central banks have worked in concert to cut key interest rates in an effort to boost economic growth.

Table 5, developed by the OECD, presents more detailed data on the tax and spending measures that are elements of the fiscal packages adopted by European countries. The data represent the value of the individual tax and spending measures represented as a share of the respective European country. The net effect represents the combination of the tax and spending measures, again represented as share of the respective country's GDP.

Table 5. Composition of Fiscal Packages of European Countries

	Net effect	Tax measures				
		Total	Individuals	Businesses	Consumption	Social contributions
Austria	−1.2	−0.8	−0.8	−0.1	0.0	0.0
Belgium	−1.4	−0.3	0.0	−0.1	−0.1	0.0
Czech Republic	−2.8	−2.5	0.0	−0.7	−0.4	−1.4
Denmark	−3.3	−0.7	0.0	0.0	0.0	0.0
Finland	−3.2	−2.7	−1.9	0.0	−0.3	−0.4
France	−0.7	−0.2	−0.1	−0.1	0.0	0.0
Germany	−3.2	−1.6	−0.6	−0.3	0.0	−0.7
Greece	0.8	0.8	0.8	0.0	0.0	0.0
Hungary	7.7	0.2	−0.6	−0.1	2.3	−1.5
Iceland	7.3	5.7	1.0	–	–	–
Ireland	8.3	6.0	4.5	−0.2	0.5	1.2
Italy	0.0	0.3	0.0	0.0	0.1	0.0
Luxembourg	−3.9	−2.3	-1.5	−0.8	0.0	0.0
Netherlands	−2.5	−1.6	-0.2	−0.5	−0.1	−0.8
Norway	−1.2	−0.3	0.0	−0.3	0.0	0.0
Poland	−1.2	−0.4	0.0	−0.1	−0.2	0.0
Portugal	−0.8	–	–	–	–	–
Slovak Republic	−1.3	−0.7	−0.5	−0.1	00	−0.1
Spain	−3.9	−1.7	−1.6	0.0	00	0.0
Sweden	−3.3	−1.7	−1.3	−0.2	0.0	−0.2
Switzerland	−0.5	−0.2	−0.2	0.0	0.0	0.0
Turkey	−4.4	−1.5	−0.2	−1.1	−0.2	0.0
United Kingdom	−1.9	−1.5	-0.5	-0.2	−0.6	0.0
	Spending measures					
	Total	Final consumption	Investment	Transfers to households	Transfers to businesses	Transfers to sub-national government
Austria	0.4	0.0	0.1	0.2	0.0	0.1
Belgium	1.1	0.0	0.1	0.5	0.5	0.0
Czech Republic	0.3	-0.1	0.2	0.0	0.2	0.0

Table 5. (Continued)

	Spending measures					
	Total	Final consumption	Investment	Transfers to households	Transfers to businesses	Transfers to sub-national government
Denmark	2.6	0.9	0.8	0.1	0.0	0.0
Finland	0.5	0.0	0.3	0.1	0.0	0.0
France	0.6	0.0	0.2	0.3	0.0	0.0
Germany	1.6	0.0	0.8	0.3	0.3	0.0
Greece	0.0	-0.4	0.1	0.4	0.1	0.0
Hungary	-7.5	-3.2	0.0	-3.4	-0.4	-0.5
Iceland	-1.6	–	–	–	–	–
Ireland	-2.2	1.8	-0.2	-0.1	0.0	0.0
Italy	0.3	0.3	0.0	0.2	0.1	0.0
Luxembourg	1.6	0.0	0.4	1.0	0.2	0.0
Netherlands	0.9	0.0	0.5	0.1	0.0	0.0
Norway	0.9	0.0	0.4	0.0	0.0	0.3
Poland	0.8	0.0	1.3	0.2	0.1	0.0
Portugal	–	0.0	0.4	0.0	0.4	0.0
Slovak Republic	0.7	0.0	0.0	0.1	0.6	0.0
Spain	2.2	0.3	0.7	0.5	0.7	0.0
Sweden	1.7	1.1	0.3	0.1	0.0	0.2
Switzerland	0.3	0.3	0.0	0.0	0.0	0.0
Turkey	2.9	0.6	1.2	0.0	0.3	0.6
United Kingdom	0.4	0.0	0.4	0.2	0.0	0.0

Source: OECD Economic Outlook, Organization for Economic Cooperation and Development, June 2009, p. 61.

Notes: Net effect represents the combination of tax measures and spending measures.

Germany

In an effort to confront worsening economic conditions, German Chancellor Angela Merkel proposed a package of stimulus measures, including spending for large-scale infrastructure projects, ranging from schools to communications. The stimulus package represents the second multi-billion euro fiscal stimulus package Germany has adopted in less than three months. The plan, announced on January 13, 2009, reportedly was doubled from initial estimates to reach more than 60 billion Euros[64] (approximately $80 billion) over two years. The plan reportedly includes a pledge by Germany's largest companies to avoid mass job cuts in return for an increase in government subsidies for employees placed temporarily on short work weeks or on lower wages.[65] Other reports indicate that Germany is considering an emergency fund of up to 100 billion Euros in state-backed loans or guarantees to aid companies having problems getting credit.[66]

Chancellor Merkel has been criticized within her own government and by other leaders in Europe for not moving aggressively enough to address either the financial crisis, or the economic downturn.[67] Initially, Merkel attempted to block and then offered tepid support for the EU plan to provide an EU-wide economic package to stimulate growth. Chancellor Merkel indicated that she has a fundamental disagreement over the effectiveness of such macroeconomic stimulus measures especially given the protracted struggle in Germany to reduce its government deficit spending to meet the guidelines in the EU Stability and Growth Pact. Instead, Merkel has argued in favor of targeted actions taken independently by EU members to tackle their own unique set of circumstances. Some observers argue that such a plan could come at a high political cost to Merkel, who vowed when she was elected to balance Germany's government budget by 2011.

Overall, Germany's response to the economic downturn changed markedly between December 2008 and January 2009 as economic conditions continued to worsen. In a December 2008 article, German Finance Minister Peer Steinbruck defended Germany's approach at the time. According to Steinbruck, Germany disagreed with the EU plan to provide a broad economic stimulus plan, because it favored an approach that is more closely tailored to the German economy. He argued that Germany is providing a counter-cyclical stimulus program even though it is contrary to its long-term goal of reducing its government budget deficit. Important to this program, however, are such "automatic stabilizers" as unemployment benefits that automatically increase without government action since such benefits play a larger role in the German economy than in other economies. Steinbruck argued that, "our experience since the 1970s has shown that ...stimulus programs fail to achieve the desired effect...It is more likely that such large-scale stimulus programs – and tax cuts as well – would not have any effects in real time. It is unclear whether general tax cuts can significantly encourage consumption during a recession, when many consumers are worried about losing their jobs. The history of the savings rate in Germany points to the opposite."[68]

France

France, which has been leading efforts to develop a coordinated European response to the financial crisis, has proposed a package of measures estimated to cost over $500 billion. The French government is creating two state agencies that will provide funds to sectors where they are needed. One entity will issue up to $480 billion in guarantees on inter-bank lending issued before December 31, 2009, and would be valid for five years. The other entity will use a $60 billion fund to recapitalize struggling companies by allowing the government to buy stakes in the firms. On January 16, 2009, President Sarkozy announced that the French government would take a tougher stance toward French banks that seek state aid. Up to that point, France had injected $15 billion in the French banking system. In order to get additional aid, banks would be required to suspend dividend payments to shareholders and bonuses to top management and to increase credit lines to such clients as exporters. France reportedly was preparing to inject more money into the banking system.[69]

On December 4, 2008, President Sarkozy announced a $33 billion (26 billion euros) package of stimulus measures to accelerate planned public investments.[70] The package is focused primarily on infrastructure projects and investments by state-controlled firms, including a canal north of Paris, renovation of university buildings, new metro cars, and construction of 70,000 new homes, in addition to 30,000 unfinished homes the government has committed to buy in 2009. The plan also includes a 200 Euro payment to low-income households. On December 15, 2008, France agreed to provide the finance division of Renault and Peugeot $1.2 billion in credit guarantees and an additional $250 million to support the car manufacturers' consumer finance division.[71] In an interview on French TV on January 14, 2009, French Prime Minister Francois Fillon indicated that the French government is considering an increase in aid to the French auto industry, including Renault and Peugeot.[72] The auto industry and its suppliers reportedly employ about 10% of France's labor force.

United Kingdom

On November 24, 2008, Britain's majority Labor party presented a plan to Parliament to stimulate the nation's slowing economy by providing a range of tax cuts and government spending projects totaling 20 billion pounds (about

$30 billion).[73] The stimulus package includes a 2.5% cut in the value added tax (VAT), or sales tax, for 13 months, a postponement of corporate tax increases, and government guarantees for loans to small and midsize businesses. The plan also includes government plans to spend 4.5 billion pounds on public works, such as public housing and energy efficiency. Some estimates indicate that the additional spending required by the plan will push Britain's government budget deficit in 2009 to an amount equivalent to 8% of GDP. To pay for the plan, the government would increase income taxes on those making more than 150,000 pounds (about $225,000) from 40% to 45% starting in April 2011. In addition, the British plan would increase the National Insurance contributions for all but the lowest income workers.[74]

On January 14, 2009, British Business Secretary Lord Mandelson unveiled an additional package of measures by the Labor government to provide credit to small and medium businesses that have been hard pressed for credit as foreign financial firms have reduced their level of activity in the UK. The three measures are: 1) a 10 billion pound (approximately $14 billion) Capital Working Scheme to provide banks with guarantees to cover 50% of the risk on existing and new working capital loans on condition that the banks must use money freed up by the guarantee to make new loans; 2) a one billion pound Enterprise Finance Guarantee Scheme to assist small, credit-worthy companies by providing guarantees to banks of up to 75% of loans to small businesses; and 3) a 75 million pound Capital for Enterprise Fund to convert debt to equity for small businesses.[75]

Prime Minister Brown has come under sharp criticism from abroad over the stimulus packages and from opposition party leaders at home over his handling of the economy before and during the financial crisis. He is also being criticized over the depreciating pound and the lack of evidence that the British economy is showing signs of responding to the economic rescue plan. German Finance Minister Peer Steinbruck, for one, called the British plan, "crass Keynesianism."[76] At home, the depreciating pound has undermined the credibility of Prime Minister Brown who previously had equated a weak currency with a weak economy and a weak government.[77] Depreciation in the exchange value of the pound puts upward pressure on domestic prices as a result of higher import prices, but it helps boost exports by reducing the cost of British goods in foreign markets.

OUTLOOK

The financial crisis has underscored the growing interdependence between financial centers and has tested the ability of EU members to cooperate in developing an EU-wide response. The financial interdependence between the United States and the European Union means that the EU and the United States share common concerns over the global impact of the financial crisis and the economic downturn. It also means that they both support and hope to benefit from efforts by national governments to stimulate their economies. Such stimulus measures, however, could become a source of friction if some of the larger economies are viewed as not carrying their share of the burden for a global recovery by providing stimulus measures that are commensurate with the size of their economy. The EU and the United States also share common concerns over the stability of East European countries. These common concerns may eventually work to spur EU members to forge a common consensus regarding the necessity of providing financial assistance to East European countries, but some observers are concerned that such a consensus may come too late to forestall serious economic deterioration in the East European economies, with implications for negative effects on the economies in Europe and the United States.

In addition to these concerns, the United States and the EU members are share common concerns over the organization of financial markets domestically and abroad and seek to improve supervision and regulation of individual institutions and of international markets. Extensive cross-border banking activities by a number of EU countries has demonstrated that serious problems in one country can have a substantial impact on the financial system elsewhere, while governments may face potentially large liabilities that are associated with branches in another country.[78] One solution that is being considered is in developing the organizational structures within national economies that can provide oversight of the different segments of the highly complex financial system. Such oversight is viewed by many as critical, because financial markets are generally considered to play an indispensible role in allocating capital and facilitating economic activity. Some observers argue, however, that the complexity of the financial system has outstripped the ability of national regulators to oversee effectively.

The financial crisis also has revealed extensive interdependency across financial market segments both within many of the advanced national financial markets and across national borders. As a result, the United States and members of the EU share mutual interests in solving both the financial crisis and the economic recession, because the two crises have become negatively reinforcing events. EU leaders are also especially concerned over the impact the economic crisis is having on the political stability and commitment to market reforms among the emerging economies of Eastern Europe. EU leaders are supporting a number of efforts to provide assistance to European economies, but they may have to expend considerably more resources if the economic crisis persists for an extended period of time.

The international nature of financial markets and capital flows likely means that efforts to address the current situation and to prevent future crisis require a coordinated response between the United States and the EU. A coordinated response likely will need to address such issues as financial market regulation, oversight of financial firms and institutions, greater transparency, and the role of independent credit rating and auditing institutions. Significant differences remain, however, among EU members and between some EU members and the United States over issues of financial supervision and regulation that could significantly complicate future efforts to craft a coordinated approach to supervising financial market at an international level. Some EU members favor a strong central authority that can monitor financial markets, while others favor strong national authorities with a weaker role for an international body. EU members recognize that economic integration means that financial and economic crises can spill across national borders, but their efforts to implement a coordinated response are being hampered by very real differences in the impact the economic recession is having on individual EU members.

The financial crisis also raises important questions about how a nation can protect its depositors from financial crisis elsewhere and about the level of financial sector debt that is manageable without risking system-wide failure. In addition, the failure of a number of large banks raises questions about bank supervision, primarily about how national governments should supervise foreign financial firms that are operating within their borders. This issue raises questions about how countries can protect their depositors when foreign-owned firms attempt to withdraw deposits from one market in order to offset losses in another. One approach focuses on broad levels of cooperation between national governments with each government addressing the crisis from its own perspective and in its own limited way. For a number of governments in Europe this approach is appealing, because their economies and their banks have felt little direct effect from the crisis.

An alternative approach argues in favor of a more integrated and coordinated response from national governments and central banks. This approach argues that a coordinated systemic approach is necessary, because financial markets in the United States and Europe have become highly integrated as a result of cross-border investment by banks, securities brokers, and other financial firms. As a result of this integration, economic and financial developments that affect national economies are difficult to contain and are quickly transmitted across national borders, as attested to by the financial crisis of 2008. As financial firms react to a financial crisis in one area, their actions can spill over to other areas as they withdraw assets from foreign markets to shore up their domestic operations. For instance, as Icelandic banks began to default, Britain used an anti-terrorism law to seize the deposits of the banks to prevent the banks from shifting funds from Britain to Iceland.[79] Banks and financial firms in Europe have felt the repercussions of the U.S. financial crisis as U.S. firms operating in Europe and as European firms operating in the United States have adjusted their operations in response to the crisis.

The financial crisis also raises questions about the cost and benefits of branch banking across national borders where banks can grow to be so large that disruptions in the financial market can cause defaults that outstrip the resources of national central banks to address. Such branch banking across national borders has significantly expanded financial opportunities for individual investors and firms alike and is unlikely to disappear as a result of the current financial crisis. Nevertheless, if some financial institutions are deemed to be too big to fail, financial regulators and national governments likely will need to address the issue of who and how such institutions should be supervised when their operations span national borders and they are engaged in a vast array of banking and investment operations.

The European Economic Recovery Plan calls for EU members to contribute an amount equal to 1.5% of their respective GDP to stimulate economic growth. Some observers argue, however, that the size of an economic stimulus package should be sufficient to address the size and nature of the relevant economic crisis, instead of being determined as a certain percentage of GDP. The nature of the current economic recession may well call for a larger stimulus package than that dictated by a pre-set percentage of a country's GDP. The ability of individual countries to provide a large economic stimulus, however, may be inhibited by actions they already have taken and by concerns over providing the right balance between sometimes competing goals of implementing policies that have a large and lasting impact but that do not threaten the long-term stability in national finances.

So far, members of the EuropeanUnion have struggled to implement a coordinated response to the economic crises. In the current context, many argue that an export-led recovery strategy is not an option. Efforts to promote exports or to discourage imports likely will not provide a significant boost to economic growth in any one country and could lead to retaliation by other countries depending on the costs and benefits of implementing such a strategy. The slowdown in economic activity has reduced exports world-wide and banks are balking at providing trade financing to small and medium firms.[80] The financial crisis also has weakened some of the traditional mechanisms through which monetary policy is transmitted. A number of EU countries already have used monetary expansion and cuts in interest rates to provide liquidity during the financial crisis and may have limited ability to provide for additional fiscal measures to stimulate their economies. Furthermore, some EU members disagree over how best to implement a coordinated economic stimulus plan, due in part to deep philosophical differences among EU members over the conduct of macroeconomic policies.

Another important factor that is affecting the EU's response to the economic recession is the need to develop new policies in a manner that meshes with the carefully crafted and highly negotiated Directives that already exist within the EU framework. These Directives act as guiding principles for EU members. In particular, the call for economic stimulus has created a conflict for some EU Members who are politically and philosophically committed to the goals of the Growth and Stability Pact and with the development goals of the Lisbon Strategy. Arguably, these agreements have helped stabilize economic conditions in Europe by bringing down the overall rate of price inflation and by reducing government budget deficits. In addition to the Lisbon Strategy, EU members likely will consider proposals to examine financial supervision and regulation within the context of the EU's Directive on Financial Services and the Financial Services Action Plan (FSAP) when it engages in negotiations with the United States and the G20 later in 2009.

APPENDIX A. OVERVIEW OF THE EUROPEAN UNION

The European Union is a political and economic union of 27 member states, formally established in 1993 by the Treaty of Maastricht out of existing structures that had evolved in steps since the 1950s. The EU has worked to develop a single economic market through a standardized system of laws which apply across all member states and which provide the freedom of movement of people, goods, services and capital. This process of economic integration is complicated by a dual system that gives the members of the EU significant independence within the EU and broad discretion to interpret and implement EU directives. The EU maintains common trade, agricultural, and fisheries policies, and a regional development policy. EU economic integration is compounded further by sixteen member states, collectively known as the Eurozone[81], which have adopted the euro as a common currency and operate as a bloc within the EU. Major institutions and bodies of the EU include: the European Commission, the European Parliament, the Council of the European Union, the European Council, the European Court of Justice, and the European Central Bank (ECB). Through various Directives, the EU has moved to increase financial integration within the Union to make the monetary union represented by the Eurozone operate more efficiently and the help the EU members realize the full potential of the EU.

Within the EU, the European Commission operates as the executive branch and is responsible for proposing legislation, implementing decisions, upholding the Union's treaties, and the general day-to-day running of the Union. The Commission operates as a cabinet government, with one Commissioner from each member. One of the 27 is the Commission President (currently José Manuel Barroso) appointed by the European Council, with the approval of the European Parliament, for a term of five years. Relative to the financial sector, the EU process provides for each member to have its own institutional and legal framework, which complicates efforts to coordinate financial policies. Within the EU, there are a number of bodies that bring together the supervisors, finance ministers, and central bankers of the EU members. Within the European Council, the Economic and Financial Affairs Council (ECOFIN) is one of the oldest bodies with the Council. ECOFIN's responsibilities include economic policy coordination, economic surveillance, monitoring of budget policy and preparation of the EU's budget. The key bodies in the EU banking sector include the following:

- **European Banking Committee.** The committee consists of representatives of the ministries of finance of the EU members and advises the EU Commission on policy issues related to banking activities and on proposals in the banking area.

- **Committee of European Banking Supervision.** The committee is comprised of representatives of supervisory authorities and central banks and coordinates on regulatory and supervisory convergence.

- **European Central Bank**. The ECB's main role is financial stability and monitoring in cooperation with national central banks and supervisory agencies.

- **Banking Supervision Committee**. This committee brings together national central banks, banking supervisory authorities, and the ECB. It monitors and assesses developments in the euro area, analyses the impact of regulatory and supervisory requirements on financial system stability, and it promotes cooperation and exchange of information between central banks and supervisory authorities on issues of common interest.

- **Economic and Financial Committee**. The committee includes representatives of ministries of finance, the European Commission, the ECB, and central banks to promote high-level assessments of developments in financial markets.

- **Financial Stability Table**. This body meets twice a year to discuss financial stability issues.

- **Financial Services Committee**. This committee is composed of representatives of the ministries of finance and the European Commission and discusses and provides guidance on cross-sector strategic and policy issues.

The euro area countries initially sketched out a broad response to the financial crisis. Since then, their response to bank foreclosures and to subsequent issues has been characterized by some as somewhat disjointed. The financial crisis and economic downturn have exposed deep fissures within the EU and even within the euro area countries over the policy course to follow. As a first response to the financial crisis, EU governments and their central banks focused policy initiatives on reassuring credit markets that there was an availability of credit and liquidity, by reducing interest rates, and by providing foreign currency, primarily dollars, through currency arrangements. In addition to continuing efforts to restore the financial markets, EU members also face a worsening economic climate that requires actions by individual central banks, international organizations, and coordinated actions by EU members and other governments.

Investment Services Directive

The EU has adopted a number of directives that provide a basic framework for EU members to coordinate financial regulation across the EU and to integrate financial sectors. One such directive is the Investment Services Directive (ISD) that entered into force on January 1, 1996. The ISD provided general principles for national securities regulations, with the goal of providing mutual recognition of regulations across the EU.[82] The ISD created a "European Passport" that provided for a cross-border right of establishment for non-bank investment firms and the freedom to provide services across borders for investment firms to carry out a wide range of investment business. Under the passport, firms were authorized and supervised by domestic authorities, but could still provide specified investment services in other EU countries. Such cross-border services included: collecting and executing buy and sell orders on an agency basis, dealing, managing and underwriting portfolios, and such additional services as providing investment advice, advising on mergers and acquisitions, safekeeping and administration of securities, and foreign exchange transactions.

The European "passport" provision required member states to dismantle restrictive legislation that prevented cross-border branching and freedom of services. Nevertheless, EU members retained the responsibility for determining their own domestic laws and regulations concerning such issues as fitness, authorization, capital requirements, and protection of client assets. EU members could also impose rules and regulations on investment firms using the European passport as long as the rules and regulations were, "in the interest of the general good," and applied to the business activities that the firms carried out in their state. The ISD opened up stock exchange membership in all member states to all types of investment firms, whether bank or non- bank entities. Another objective of the ISD was to eliminate the so-called concentration rule in order to allow member states that lacked their own securities trading floor to access electronic terminals with investment firms and banks in other member states, thereby allowing them to be members of the markets on a remote electronic basis.

Financial Services Action Plan

In 1999, the EU replaced the Investment Services Directive with the Financial Services Action Plan. The Plan consists of a set of measures that are intended to remove the remaining formal barriers in financial markets among EU members and to provide a legal and regulatory environment that supports the integration of EU financial markets.[83] Similar to the ISD, the FSAP process supports a two-pronged approach that combines EU directives with national laws. The EU directives provide for a general level of regulation concerning the provision of financial services across borders and the harmonization of national regulations governing cross-border activities. EU members, however, retain the right to regulate firms within their own borders, as long as those firms, whether foreign or domestic, are treated equally. The FSAP contains 42 articles, 38 of which were implemented, that are intended to meet three specific objectives: 1) a single wholesale market; 2) an open and secure retail market; and 3) state-of-the art rules and supervision. Wholesale measures relate to securities issuance and trading; securities settlement; accounts; and corporate restructuring. Retail measures relate to insurance; savings through pension funds and mutual funds; retail payments; electronic money; and money laundering.

Markets in Financial Instruments Directive

The cornerstone of the FSAP's achievement is the Markets in Financial Instruments Directive (MiFID), which became effective on November 1, 2007. The MiFID establishes a comprehensive, harmonized set of rules for Europe's securities markets so financial services firms can provide investment services in each of the EU member states. MiFID retained the principles of the EU "passport" and extended the list of services and financial instruments that are covered by the passport procedures, including investment advice. MiFID also removed the so-called concentration rule that required investment firms to route all stock transactions through established exchanges.

MiFID introduced the concept of 'maximum harmonization' which places more emphasis on home state supervision. This is a change from the previous EU financial service legislation which featured a "minimum harmonization and mutual recognition" concept. Minimum harmonization provides for a law or a regulation that sets a floor, or a minimum standard, that EU countries were expected to meet in developing legislation. Maximum harmonization provides for a maximum level of a law or a regulation that sets the maximum allowable standard that can be adopted in domestic laws or regulations. At times some EU members have been accused of adopting domestic measures that exceed the EU standard in a manner that acted as a protectionist barrier.

Some key elements of the MiFID are:

- Authorization, regulation and passporting. Firms covered by MiFID are authorized and regulated in their "home state." Once a firm is authorized, it can use the MiFID passport to provide services to customers in other EU member states. These services are regulated by the "home state" in which the firm is authorized.
- Client categorization. MiFID requires firms to categorize clients as "eligible counter-parties," professional clients, or retail clients, with increasing levels of protection.
- Client order handling. MiFID places requirements on information that needs to be captured when firms accept client orders in order to ensure that a firm is acting in a client's best interests.
- Pre-trade transparency. MiFID requires the operators of various kinds of equity exchanges to make the best bid and offer prices available to potential buyers and sellers.
- Post-trade transparency. MiFID requires firms to publish the price, volume and time of all trades in listed shares, even if executed outside of a regulated market, unless certain requirements are met to allow for deferred publication.
- Best execution. MiFID will require that firms take all reasonable steps to obtain the best possible result in the execution of an order for a client. The best possible result is not limited to execution price but also includes cost, speed, likelihood of execution and likelihood of settlement and any other factors deemed relevant.
- Systematic Internalizer. A Systematic Internalizer is a firm that executes orders from its clients against its own book or against orders from other clients and are treated as mini-exchanges, which makes them subject to pre-trade and post-trade transparency requirements

Capital Requirements Directive

The Capital Requirements Directive, which became effective in January 2007, introduced a supervisory framework within the EU for investment management firms and banks. The purpose of the Directive is to move the EU towards complying with the Basel II[84] rules on capital measurement, adequacy, and related market disclosure disciplines. This Directive promotes a risk based capital management methodology through a "three pillar" structure that includes: 1) new standards that set out the minimum capital requirements that firms will be required to meet for credit, market, and operational risk; 2) firms and supervisors will be required to decide whether they are holding enough capital to address the risks realized under Pillar I and act accordingly; and 3) improve market discipline by requiring firms to publish certain details about their risks, capital, and risk management. The Directive also requires firms to make provision for a charge against their capital for operational risks in order to identify, monitor, manage, and report on certain types of external events that may have a negative effect on their capital. The Directive applies not only to internationally active banks, which is the main focus of the Basel II approach, but it also applies to all credit institutions and investment firms irrespective of the size, scope of activities, or levels of sophistication. Under the Directive, firms are required to meet rules governing the minimum amounts of their own financial resources they must have in order to cover the risks to which they may be exposed.

Lamfalussy Process

As the European Commission crafted a coordinated EU approach to the financial crisis, it has done so in accordance with a set of procedures known as the Lamfalussy Process. The Lamfalussy structure provides a framework for updating EU financial regulations and developing similar supervisory practices. While this process can be time consuming, it provides a process for EU members to follow so that policies that are considered through the process ultimately will be acceptable to all EU members and, therefore, will be more likely to be implemented. MiFID is the most significant piece of legislation that has been introduced under this process. Originally developed in March of 2001, it is named after the chair of the EU advisory committee that created it, Alexandre Lamfalussy. The process is composed of four "levels," each focusing on a specific stage of the implementation of legislation. Level 1 is traditional EU decision making, which means that decisions are adopted in the form of Directives or Regulations proposed by the Commission and then approved under the co-decision procedure by the European Parliament and the EU Council. Legislation adopted at this level primarily establishes the core values of a law.

At the second level, sector-specific committees and regulators provide advice on developing the technical details of the principles that were adopted in Level 1 and then bring the measure to a vote by the representatives of each

EU member. These measures can be adopted, adapted and updated by the Commission after they have been submitted to the European Securities Committee (ESC), a committee composed mainly of members of Ministries of Finance, and to the European Parliament for their opinion. The Committee of European Securities Regulators (CESR), an independent advisory body made up of securities regulators, also advises the Commission on the technical implementing details to be included in Level 2 legislation. This advice is provided in response to specific "mandates" from the Commission asking for help in particular areas. Level 2 implementing measures do not alter the principles agreed upon at Level 1, but simply provide the technical details that are necessary in order to make the principles operational.

At the third level, national regulators work on coordinating new regulations with other nations. At this stage, CESR may adopt non-binding guidelines or common standards regarding matters not covered by EU legislation, as long as these standards are compatible with the legislation adopted at Level 1 and Level 2.

The fourth level involves compliance and enforcement of the new rules and laws, including initiating proceedings on cases of non-conformity.

The Lamfalussy Process is intended to provide several benefits over traditional lawmaking, including more-consistent interpretation, convergence in national supervisory practices, and a general boost in the quality of legislation on financial services. Nevertheless, the Lamfalussy Process has sparked controversy, because some critics argue that the procedure can effectively bypass accountable oversight by the European Council and the elected European Parliament, thereby embodying a move away from representative democracy towards technocratic and participatory democracy.

End Notes

[1] Members of the European Union are: Austria, Belgium, Bulgaria, Cyprus, the Czech Republic, Denmark, Estonia, Finland, France, Germany, Greece, Hungary, Ireland, Italy, Latvia, Lithuania, Luxembourg, Malta, the Netherlands, Poland, Portugal, Romania, Slovakia, Slovenia, Spain, Sweden, and the United Kingdom.

[2] Blair, Dennis C., *Annual Threat Assessment of the Intelligence Community for the Senate Select Committee on Intelligence*, February 12, 2009.

[3] Members of the Euro area have adopted the Euro as their common currency. Member countries are: Austria, Belgium, Cyprus, Finland, France, Germany, Greece, Ireland, Italy, Luxembourg, Malta, the Netherlands, Portugal, Slovakia, Slovenia, and Spain.

[4] Pan, Phillip P., Economic Crisis Fuels Unrest in E. Europe, *The Washington Post*, January 26, 2009, p, A1.

[5] Shin, Annys, World Bank to Offer Aid to Eastern Europe, *The Washington Post*, February 27, 2009, p. A10.

[6] To join the Eurozone, countries must keep their government budget deficits, their overall level of government debt, and the rate of price inflation below specified fixed ceilings and hold their currencies within a preset range to the Euro for two years.

[7] Forelle, Charles, EU Rejects a Rescue of Faltering East Europe, *The Wall Street Journal*, March 2, 2009.

[8] Bryant, Chris, EU Leaders Push Sweeping Regulations, *Financial Times*, February 22, 2009.

[9] *Report*, The High-Level Group on Financial Supervision in the EU, Chaired by Jacques de Larosiere, February 25, 2009.

[10] *Driving European Recovery*, Communication for the Spring European Council, Commission of the European Communities, April 3, 2009.

[11] Level 3 committees represent the third level of the Lamfalussy process the EU uses to implement EU-wide policies. At the third level, national regulators work on coordinating new regulations with other nations. and they may adopt non-binding guidelines or common standards regarding matters not covered by EU legislation, as long as these standards are compatible with the legislation adopted at Level 1 and Level 2.

[12] *A European Economic Recovery Plan*: Communication From the Commission to the European Council, Commission of the European Communities, COM(2008) 800 final, November 26, 2008. The full report is available at: http://ec.europa.eu/commission_barroso/president/pdf/Comm_20081126.pdf

[13] *EU Banking Structures*, European Central Bank, October 2008.

[14] The Stability and Growth Pact (SGP) is an agreement by European Union members to conduct their fiscal policy in a manner that facilitates and maintains the Economic and Monetary Union of the European Union. The Pact was adopted in 1997 and is based on Articles 99 and 104 of the European Community Treaty, or the Maastricht Treaty, and related decisions. It consists of monitoring the fiscal policies of the members by the European Commission and the Council so that fiscal discipline is maintained and enforced in the Economic and Monetary Union (EMU). The actual criteria that members states must respect are: 1) an annual budget deficit no higher than 3% of GDP, and 2) a national debt lower than 60% of GDP, or approaching that value.

[15] The Lisbon Strategy for Growth and Jobs is a plan adopted by EU members to improve economic growth and employment among the EU members by becoming the most competitive knowledge based economy in the world by 2010. The comprehensive strategy includes adopting sustainable macroeconomic policies, business friendly regulatory and tax policies and benefits, improved education and training, and greater investment in energy efficient and environmentally friendly technology. Two major goals include total public and private investment of 3% of Europe's GDP in research and employment by 2010, and an employment rate of 70% by the same date. A comprehensive report on the Lisbon Strategy is available at: http://ec.europa.EU/growthandjobs/pdf/kok_report_en.pdf.

[16] The Financial Services Action Plan replaced the Investment Services Directive and contains a set of measures that are intended to remove the remaining formal barriers in the financial services market among EU members and to provide a legal and regulatory environment that supports the integration of the EU financial markets. *The EU Financial Services Action Plan: A Guide*, HM Treasury, the Financial Services authority, and the Bank of England, July 31, 2003.

[17] Flash Estimates for the Fourth Quarter of 2008, Eurostat news release, STAT/09/19, February 13, 2009.

[18] See CRS Report R40 173, *Causes of the Financial Crisis*, by Mark Jickling; CRS Report R40007, *Financial Market Turmoil and U.S. Macroeconomic Performance*, by Craig K. Elwell; CRS Report RL34412, *Containing Financial Crisis*, by Mark Jickling; CRS Report RS22963, *Financial Market Intervention*, by Edward V. Murphy and Baird Webel; and

CRS Report RL34742, *The Global Financial Crisis: Analysis and Policy Implications*, coordinated by Dick K. Nanto.

[19] Fender, Ingo, and Jacob Gyntelberg, Overview: Global Financial Crisis Spurs Unprecedented Policy Actions, *BIS Quarterly Review*, Bank for International Settlements, December 2008.

[20] *Regional Economic Outlook: Europe*, International Monetary Fund, April, 2008, p. 19-20; and *EU Banking Structures*, European Central Bank, October 2008, p. 26.

[21] Commercial paper is a short-term unsecured money market security with a fixed maturity issued by large banks and corporations to get money to meet short-term debt obligations and is only backed by an issuing bank or corporation's promise to pay the face amount on the maturity date. Asset-backed commercial paper is a form of commercial paper that is collateralized by other financial assets.

[22] CRS ReportRS22988, *Iceland's Financial Crisis*, by James K. Jackson.

[23] Anderson, Camilla, Iceland Gets Help to Recover From Historic Crisis, *IMF Survey Magazine*, November 19, 2008.

[24] Credit default swaps are insurance-like contracts that promise to cover losses on certain securities in the event of a default. They typically apply to municipal bonds, corporate debt and mortgage securities and are sold by banks, hedge funds, and others. The buyer of the credit default insurance pays premiums over a period of time in return for peace of mind, knowing that losses will be covered if a default happens. They are supposed to work similarly to someone taking out home insurance to protect against losses from fire and theft.

[25] *Regional Economic Outlook: Europe*, International Monetary Fund, November,2007, p. 6.; and *Quarterly Review*, Bank for International Settlements, December, 2008. p. 4.

[26] Chailloux, Alexandre, Simon Gray, Ulrich Kluh, Seiichi Shimizu, and Peter Stella, *Central Bank Response to the 2007-08 Financial Market Turbulence: Experiences and Lessons Drawn*. IMF Working Paper wP/08/210, International Monetary Fund, September 2008.

[27] Bernanke, Ben S., *Liquidity Provision by the Federal Reserve*, May 13, 2008.

[28] Borio, Claudio, and William Nelson, Monetary Operations and the Financial Crisis, *Quarterly Review*, March 2008, Bank for International Settlements.

[29] The Special Liquidity Scheme was launched by the Bank of England on April 21, 2008, to allow banks to temporarily swap their high-quality mortgage-backed and other securities for UK Treasury bills. A number of features of the program are: the swap of government securities will be for one year, but renewable at the Bank of England's discretion for up to three years; the Treasury securities will be available with a fee based on the spread between the LIBOR (the London Interbank Offer Rate) rate and the rate on certain government bonds; risks on the mortgage securities remains with the banks and the banks are required to use only rated assets as collateral; the swaps are available only for assets that were on the bank's balance sheets at the end of 2007 and cannot be used to finance new lending, and the assets of the banks are subject to valuation by the Bank of England; securities provided by the Bank of England are to be marketable Treasury securities that the banks can choose to hold, use as part of the Bank of England's standard market operations, or swap them for cash; the scheme will be closed down by October 2011 with all Treasury securities returned to the Bank of England; and the scheme will not be independent of the Bank of England's monetary policy actions.

[30] *Financial Stability Report*, April 2008, Bank of England. P. 10

[31] Ibid., p. 31.

[32] *Summit of the Euro Area Countries: Declaration on a Concerted European Action Plan of the Euro Area Countries*, European Union, October 12, 2008.

[33] *EU Sets up Crisis Unit to Boost Financial Oversight*, Thompson Financial News, October 16, 2008.

[34] *Ibid*.

[35] Bradbury, Adam, EU Eyes Next Step on Clearing *The Wall Street Journal Europe*, January 7, 2009. P. 21.

[36] Hilsenrath, Jon, Joellen Perry, and Sudeep Reddy, Central Banks Launch Coordinated Attack; Emergency Rate Cuts Fail to Halt stock Slide; U.S. Treasury Considers Buying Stakes in Banks as Direct Move to Shore Up Capital, *The Wall Street Journal*, October 8, 2008, p. A1.

[37] The original eight banks are: Bank of America, Bank of New York Mellon Corporation, Citigroup Incorporated, Goldman Sachs Group Incorporated, JPMorgan Chase & Company, Morgan Stanley, State Street Corporation, and Wells Fargo and Company. Since this initial injection, nearly 50 banks have participated in the Capital Purchase Program.

[38] Hilsenrath, Jon, Joellen Perry, and Liz Rappaport, Fed Steps up Assault on Slump; U.S. is Joined in Rate Cuts by China, Norway; Doubts Linger on Easing's Impact, *The Wall Street Journal*, October 30, 2008, p. A1.

[39] Atkins, Ralph, and Chris Giles, Deep Rate Cuts in Europe, *Financial Times*, November 7, 2008, p. 1.

[40] Atkins, Ralph, ECB Acts and Hints at More to Come Soon, *Financial Times*, November 7, 2008, p. 2.

[41] *78th Annual Report*, Bank for International Settlements, p. 104-105.

[42] The central banks include: Swiss National Bank, European Central Bank, Bank of England, Bank of Japan, Bank of Canada, Reserve Bank of Australia, Sveriges Riksbank (Sweden), National Bank of Denmark, Central Bank of Norway, Reserve Bank of Norway, Reserve Bank of New Zealand, Central Bank of Brazil, Bank of Mexico, Bank of Korea, Monetary Authority of Singapore, Swiss National Bank, and National Bank of Poland.

[43] The G-7 is comprised of Canada, France, Germany, Italy, Japan, the United Kingdom, and the United States.

[44] *G-7 Finance Ministers and Central Bank Governors Plan of Action*, press release HP-1 195, October 10, 2008, United States Department of the Treasury.

[45] Summit of the Euro Area Countries: Declaration on a Concerted European Action Plan of the Euro Area Countries, European Union, October 12, 2008.

[46] Perry, Joellen, and Marcus Walker, Europe's Central Banks Deliver Sweeping Rate Cuts, *Financial Times*, December 5, 2008. P. 1.

[47] Bank of England Reduces Bank Rate by 0.5 Percentage Points to 1.5%, Bank of England news release, January 8, 2009.

[48] *Bank of England Reduces Bank Rate by 0.5 Percentage Points to 1.0%*, Bank of England news release, February 5, 2009.

[49] Perry, Joellen, Nicholas Winning, and Joe Parkinson, Euro-Zone Activity Slows – Large ECB Rate Cut Expected After Data on Inflation, Services, *The Wall Street Journal Europe*, January 7, 2009. P. 2; Statement by Jean-Claude Trichet, European Central Bank, January 15, 2009.

[50] Statement by Jean-Claude Trichet.

[51] The TARP funds have been used instead to inject capital directly into banks through purchases of newly-issued preferred stock.

[52] *Financial Stability Plan Fact Sheet*, U.S. Department of the Treasury, news release, February 9, 2009.

[53] *From Financial Crisis to Recovery: A European Framework for Action*, Communication From the Commission, European Commission, COM(2008) 706 final, October 29, 2008.

[54] The combination of labor market flexibility and security for workers.

[55] The Stability and Growth Pact (SGP) is an agreement by European Union members to conduct their fiscal policy in a manner that facilitates and maintains the Economic and Monetary Union of the European Union. The Pact was adopted in 1997 and is based on Articles 99 and 104 of the European Community Treaty, or the Maastricht Treaty, and related decisions. It consists of monitoring the fiscal policies of the members by the European Commission and the Council so that fiscal discipline is maintained and enforced in the European Monetary Union (EMU). The actual criteria that member states must respect are

1) an annual budget deficit no higher than 3% of GDP, and 2) a national debt lower than 60% of GDP or approaching that value.

[56] The European Social Fund, created in 1957, is the EU's main financial instrument for assisting members in implementing their own plans for investing in workers.

[57] Hall, Ben, George Parker, and Nikki Tait, European Leaders Decide on Deadline for Reform Blueprint, *Financial Times*, November 8, 2008, p. 7.

[58] *Principles for Sound Stress Testing Practices and Supervision*: Consultative Document, Bank for International Settlements, January 2009.

[59] Munoz, Sara Schaefer, and Alistair MacDonald, U.K. Weighs "Bad Banks," *The Wall Street Journal Europe*, February 4, 2009, p. 2.

[60] Perry, Joellen, and Marcus Walker, Central Bank Mulls "Bad Banks," *The Wall Street Journal Europe*, February 2, 2009, p. 19.

[61] CRS Report RS22850, *Tax Provisions of the 2008 Economic Stimulus Package*, coordinated by Jane G. Gravelle.

[62] Dougherty, Carter, British Central Bank Cuts Its Key Rate, *The New York Times*, March 6, 2009; *March 5, 2009 – Monetary Policy Decisions*, press release, the European Central Bank.

[63] *A European Economic Recovery Plan*: Communication From the Commission to the European Council, Commission of the European Communities, COM(2008) 800 final, November 26, 2008. The full report is available at: http://ec.europa.eu/commission_barroso/president/pdf/Comm_20081126.pdf

[64] Benoit, Bernard, Germany Doubles Size of Stimulus, *Financial Times*, January 6, 2009, p. 10; Walker, Marcus, Germany's Big Spending Plans, *The Wall Street Journal Europe*, January 13, 2009, p. 3.

[65] Benoit, Bernard, German Stimulus Offers Job Promise, *Financial Times*, December 16, 2008. p. 1.

[66] Walker, Marcus, Germany Mulls $135 Billion in Rescue Loans, *The Wall Street Journal Europe*, January 8, 2009. p. 1.

[67] Benoit, Bernard, A Measured Merkel, *Financial Times*, November 25, 2008, p. 9.

[68] Steinbruck, Peer, Germany's Way Out of the Crisis, *The Wall Street Journal*, December 22, 2008.

[69] Parussini, Gabrielle, France to Give Banks Capital, With More Strings Attached, *The Wall Street Journal Europe*, January 16, 2009, p. A17.

[70] Gauthier-Villars, David, Leading News: France Sets Stimulus Plan, *The Wall Street Journal Europe*, December 5, 2008, p. 3.

[71] Hall, Ben, France Gives Renault and Peugeot E.U.R 779m, *Financial Times*, December 16, 2008, p. 4.

[72] Abboud, Leila, France Considers New Measures to Aid Auto Companies, *The Wall Street Journal Europe*, January 15, 2009, p. 4.

[73] Scott, Mark, Is Britain's Stimulus Plan a Wise Move? *Business Week*, November 24, 2008; Werdigier, Julia, Britain Offers $30 Billion Stimulus Plan, *The New York Times*, November 25, 2008.

[74] Falloon, Matt, and Mike Peacock, UK Government to Borrow Record Sums to Revive Economy, *The Washington Post*, November 24, 2008.

[75] *Real Help for Business*, press release, Department for Business, Enterprise and Regulatory Reform, January 14, 2009; Mollenkamp, Carrick, Alistair MacDonald, and Sara Schaefer Munoz, Hurdles rise as U.K. Widens Stimulus Plan, *The Wall Street Journal Europe*, January 14, 2009, p. 1.

[76] Watt, Nicholas, British Ambassador Responds to German Economic Criticism, *Guardian*, December 12, 2008.

[77] Parker, George, Brown Suffers as Pound Slides, *Financial Times*, December 16, 2008, p. 9.

[78] *OECD Economic Surveys: Europe*, January 2009, Organization for Economic Cooperation and Development, p. 47.

[79] Benoit, Bertrand, Tom Braithwaaite, Jimmy Burns, Jean Eaglesham, et. al., Iceland and UK clash on Crisis, Financial Times, October 10, 2008, p. 1.

[80] Evans, Kelly, John W. Milner, and Mei Fong, Trade Decline Adds to the Global Slowdown – Major Nations Post Big Export Retreats as Demand Falls Off, *The Wall Street Journal Europe*, January 14, 2009, p. 2; Lyons, John, Trade- Finance Squeeze Hurts the Healthy, *The Wall Street Journal Europe*, December 22, 2008, p. 10.

[82] Davies, Ryan J., *MiFID and a Changing Competitive Landscape*, July 2008., p. 3. Available online at: http://faculty.babson.edu/rdavies/MiFID_July2008_Davies15.pdf

[83] *The EU Financial Services Action Plan: A Guide*, HM Treasury, the Financial Services Authority, and the Bank of England, July 31, 2003.

[84] Basel II is the second of the Basel Accords, which are recommendations on banking laws and regulations issued by the Basel Committee on Banking Supervision. The purpose of Basel II is to create an international standard that banking regulators can use when creating regulations concerning requirements for capital adequacy that banks must meet to guard against the types of financial and operational risks that banks face.

In: European Response to the Financial Crisis   ISBN: 978-1-60876-817-2
Editor: Baron L. Whitley   © 2010 Nova Science Publishers, Inc.

Chapter 3

THE U.S. FINANCIAL CRISIS: LESSONS FROM SWEDEN[*]

James K. Jackson

SUMMARY

In the early 1990s, Sweden faced a banking and exchange rate crisis that led it to rescue banks that had experienced large losses on their balance sheets and that threatened a collapse of the banking system. Some analysts and others argue that Sweden's experience could provide useful lessons for the execution and implementation of the Emergency Economic Stabilization Act of 2008[1]. The banking crisis facing the United States is unique, so there are no exact parallels from which to draw templates. Sweden's experience, however, represents a case study in how a systemic banking crisis was resolved in a developed country with democratic institutions. The Swedish central bank separated out good assets, which it left to the banks to oversee from bad assets, which it placed in a separate agency with broad authority to work out debt problems or to liquidate assets. Four lessons that emerged form Sweden's experience are: 1) the process must be transparent; 2) the resolution agency must be politically and financially independent; 3) market discipline must be maintained; and 4) there must be a plan to jump-start credit flows in the financial system. This report provides an overview of the Swedish banking crisis and an explanation of the measures Sweden used to restore its banking system to health. This report will not be updated.

BACKGROUND

Sweden's banking crisis grew slowly over time and was the result of a number of policy decisions[2]. In particular, the crisis arose from a set of economic policies that attempted to: 1) support Sweden's fixed exchange rate policy, 2) deregulate the financial sector, 3) expand credit, and 4) provide low-cost loans for residential purchases and for university students. Eventually, a drop in asset values weakened the balance sheets of banks and reduced liquidity in the economy. One key factor in Sweden's financial crisis was a set of policy measures the country adopted in the mid-1980s to liberalize the highly regulated financial sector. Prior to this liberalization, banks, insurance companies, and other institutions were subjected to lending ceilings and were required to invest in bonds issued by the government and mortgage institutions.

Large central government deficits and a national policy that favored residential investment led to requirements that banks hold more than 50% of their assets in such bonds, typically with long maturities and low interest rates. In addition, the banks were carefully scrutinized and monitored by Riksbank, Sweden's central bank. This close supervision meant, however, that the banks themselves were unaccustomed to performing risk analysis, and were ill-prepared to perform risk analysis on commercial paper associated with real estate loans. This lack of experience led to unhealthy risk taking when the nation began to deregulate its financial sector and allow banks to participate in a broader array of financial instruments. Indeed, some analysts argue that it was this inexperience, rather than the deregulation effort itself, that played a role in the banking crisis. Sweden also favored housing and college education by operating a system that provided loans with highly favorable terms with little or no credit evaluation. Other economic problems compounded Sweden's efforts to gain control over the macroeconomic conditions within the country and place the economy on a well-balanced positive growth track[3].

---

[*] This is an edited, reformatted and augmented version of a Congressional Research Service Report RS22962, dated September 29, 2008.

DEREGULATION

In the early to mid-1980s, Sweden began deregulating its financial markets at such a rapid pace that it took most observers by surprise[4]. In part the deregulation was spurred by the rapid development that had occurred in the growth of money market accounts, certificates of deposit, and government securities that arose from growing central government budget deficits. These actions shifted Sweden's monetary policy to an expansive posture and allowed banks, mortgage institutions, finance companies, and others to compete in the domestic credit market. The expansion in credit helped stimulate economic growth, but it also fed inflation and added to general expectations of inflation in the economy. In addition, Sweden's tax system stimulated consumer borrowing by allowing taxpayers to fully deduct interest payments and exchange controls stimulated corporate borrowing by favoring domestic investment over foreign investment.

These activities combined with an expansionary fiscal policy to increase credit in the economy added to the stock, or the overall amount, of debt. This credit boom pushed up the prices of corporate stocks and real estate—both commercial real estate and residential housing. As the pace of economic growth accelerated, the rate of price inflation also increased, which led to the Swedish Krona being overvalued. By the late 1980s, Sweden removed a broad range of foreign exchange controls, but it maintained its fixed exchange rate system. During this time, Sweden experienced current account deficits and large outflows of direct investment and other long-term capital, which led to a growing stock of private sector short-term debt in foreign currency[5]. In essence, Swedish households and businesses were borrowing in foreign currency at interest rates that were below those that were charged for loans denominated in Swedish Krona. The result of this borrowing was a substantial amount of exchange rate risk in the balance sheets of the private sector.

By the early 1990s, a combination of reforms in the tax system and periods of high interest rates caused asset prices to fall. As the pace of economic growth cooled, the rate of unemployment began to rise, public sector debt rose, bankruptcies surged, and the banking system was shocked as the rising bankruptcies forced banks to curtail their lending activities in order to build up their loan loss reserves. A further setback for the economy occurred with German reunification in 1990, which resulted in higher German interest rates and an appreciating currency. Sweden's fixed exchange rate policy obligated Sweden to import the higher German interest rates, pushing its own interest rates higher and busting a property market bubble. When

Sweden was forced to abandon its exchange rate peg in November 1992, the real exchange rate fell substantially, while real interest rates remained high, which caused a large number of private sector loans to become non-performing.

THE FINANCIAL CRISIS

In early 1990, Sweden's economy appeared to be doing well. The unemployment rate was at an all-time low and the stock market was booming. At the same time, the rate of price inflation was rising, the real effective exchange rate was appreciating, and there was a general consensus that the economy was growing at an unsustainable rate. In addition, rising stock market prices reinforced the continued expansion in real estate, especially in the commercial property market. By mid-1990, however, commercial occupancy rates had fallen, pushing down the price of stocks for both the real estate and construction sectors[6].

The first financial firm to feel the effects of the drop in real estate prices was Nyckeln, one of Sweden's fastest growing financial firms. Nyckeln, like other financial firms, was owned by several of Sweden's largest banks. Nyckeln had achieved its rapid growth by specializing in commercial real estate financing and financing its operations through a new type of commercial paper called marknadsbevis, which the banks had guaranteed. At this time, Sweden's commercial paper market had become the third largest commercial paper market in Europe. In 1991, the value of commercial paper dropped sharply when interest rates in Sweden began rising as a result of rising international rates that were pushed up by German reunification. With the fall of Nyckeln, two of Sweden's six largest banks were heavily affected and announced that they could not meet their regulatory capital requirements.

Concern quickly spread through all of Sweden's commercial paper market, which essentially shut down. By the end of the year, three of Sweden's major financial firms had defaulted. Two of the major banks faced actual insolvency problems and the government of Sweden, the major shareholder in the two banks, injected equity into one of the banks and issued guarantees to the other bank for loans that enabled the banks to fulfill their capital requirements. By the spring of 1992, yet another Swedish bank went bankrupt. At this point, the Swedish government took ownership of the third bank and began to treat the defaults and bankruptcy as a crisis. The government refused to offer complete forbearance of the non-performing loans and did not offer unlimited liquidity support, but opted to guarantee the bank's debts, an action it would extend to all of Sweden's banks within a few weeks.

As a major step in resolving the banking crisis, the central bank divided each bank into two separate entities, one with its good assets, the other with its bad assets. The entities holding the good assets continued to operate under their old names and were later merged under a new name. The bad assets were transferred to two asset management companies. The asset management companies were owned by the government, but had a high degree of independence and were free of many of the regulations that applied to banks. The management companies attempted to assess the value of the non-performing loans they had inherited and then moved to rescue whatever economic value they could. As a result, the companies injected equity into troubled borrowers to maintain and restore their values and, at times, took over defaulting companies, which they ran as a private owner until the companies could be liquidated. Assets were sold in three ways: initial public offerings on the Stockholm stock exchange; corporate transaction outside the stock exchange; and transactions involving individual properties. A quick rebound in the Swedish economy that stemmed from an increase in economic growth in Europe and elsewhere allowed all of the managed assets to be liquidated by 1997, ultimately at a lower cost to the Swedish taxpayers than had initially been projected.

LESSONS LEARNED FROM SWEDEN'S EXPERIENCE

Each financial crisis is unique and largely dependent on the specific combination of national and international factors that exist at the time. In addition, the resolution of the crisis is intricately interwoven with a broad set of laws and national characteristics that are unique to each crisis and each national setting. A number of differences between the Swedish and U.S. experiences are readily apparent.

- Unlike the situation in the United States, the Swedish government had a financial stake in the largest banks prior to the crisis. This made the Swedish government a direct stakeholder in the institutions and provided an impetus for it to act.

- Sweden's real estate loans and commercial paper were nearly all domestically held, so that it did not face both a domestic and international financial issue.
- Many nonperforming loans in Sweden were a result of unhedged private sector exchange rate risk when the currency peg collapsed.
- In the United States, the financial sector problems are linked to the
- securitization of mortgages, which led to credit exposures that extended well beyond the retail banking sector.
- Sweden's economy is small and open, which enables it to rely on an export-led recovery strategy. The U.S. economy is larger relative to the global economy and it has a strong influence on the pace of global economic growth. As a result, the United States is more likely to rely on a recovery strategy that is based on domestic demand.

An analysis of the Swedish banking crisis of the 1990s reveals that there are a number of factors that were inherently responsible for the resolution of the crisis that apply specifically to the Swedish case. Despite these caveats, the Swedish experience may offer some insight into one possible way of resolving a domestic financial crisis. One factor that helped Sweden quickly resolve its financial crisis was a strong international economic recovery that pushed up real estate values in Sweden and improved the balance sheets of banks. Others argue that a number of procedural factors, in addition to the economic recovery, helped bring the financial crisis to a resolution. In particular, they argue that four factors played an important role in this process in Sweden and could prove beneficial in resolving other financial crises:[7]

- First, transparency of the process is important. In Sweden, expected losses were recognized early on and helped to preserve the confidence of the market.
- Second, the process seems to work best with a politically and financially independent agency. This type of structure shields decision makers from political pressures, especially as banks are closed and assets are liquidated. Financial independence of the agency gives credibility to the notion of political independence. In addition, financial independence allows for a rapid response when funding needs emerge suddenly and waiting for a government appropriation is impractical.
- Third, is the importance of maintenance of market discipline and avoiding blanket guarantees. According to this concept, extending

blanket guarantees increases the risk of future financial crisis because it weakens market discipline exerted by uninsured creditors. Blanket guarantees of all the liabilities of problem institutions in the throes of a crisis reduces the credibility of claims that such guarantees will not be extended in future bank failures. Although the guarantees were intended to calm the markets, some analysts argue they likely reduced incentives to monitor bank risk by creditors. Some analysts argue that a better solution would be a bank holiday that would allow bank examiners enough time to assess the extent of non-performing loans while it would allow insured depositors access to their funds. In addition, uninsured depositors would be allowed to move their funds out, but would be forced to assume some of the losses. Also non-viable banks would not be eligible to receive financial support from the government and public funds would not be used to support a non-viable institution.

- Fourth, is a plan to jump-start credit flows in the financial system by repairing the damaged creditworthiness of the broader economy. Even if banks can be completely restored to financial health through recapitalization, borrowers may be in no position to repay any new loans they may get. Such a plan may include such items as a fiscal stimulus to aid borrowers.

End Notes

[1] Dougherty, Carter, Stopping a Financial Crisis, The Swedish Way, *The New York Times*, September 23, 2008; Purvis, Andrew, Sweden's Model Approach to Financial Disaster, *Time*, September 24, 2008.
[2] Englund, Peter, The Swedish Banking Crisis: Roots and Consequences, *Oxford Review of Economic Policy,* Autumn 1999. P. 80-97.
[3] Ibid, p. 83-84.
[4] Ingves, Stefan, *The Nordic Banking Crisis From an International Perspective*, International Monetary Fund, September 11, 2002.
[5] Backstrom, Urban, *What Lessons Can be Learned From Recent Financial Crises? The Swedish Experience.* Federal Reserve Symposium "Maintaining Financial Stability in a global Economy," August 29, 1997.
[6] Englund, The Swedish Banking Crisis, p. 84-89.
[7] Ergungor, O. *Emre, On the Resolution of Financial Crises: The Swedish Experience*, Federal Reserve Bank of Cleveland Policy Discussion Paper, June 2007, p. 1-12.

In: European Response to the Financial Crisis ISBN: 978-1-60876-817-2
Editor: Baron L. Whitley © 2010 Nova Science Publishers, Inc.

Chapter 4

ICELAND'S FINANCIAL CRISIS[*]

James K. Jackson

SUMMARY

On November 19, 2008, Iceland and the International Monetary Fund (IMF) finalized an agreement on a $6 billion economic stabilization program supported by a $2.1 billion loan from the IMF. Following the IMF decision, Denmark, Finland, Norway, and Sweden agreed to provide an additional $2.5 billion. Iceland's banking system had collapsed as a culmination of a series of decisions the banks made that left them highly exposed to disruptions in financial markets. The collapse of the banks also raises questions for U.S. leaders and others about supervising banks that operate across national borders, especially as it becomes increasingly difficult to distinguish the limits of domestic financial markets. Such supervision is important for banks that are headquartered in small economies, but operate across national borders. If such banks become so overexposed in foreign markets that a financial disruption threatens the solvency of the banks, the collapse of the banks can overwhelm domestic credit markets and outstrip the ability of the central bank to serve as the lender of last resort. This report will be updated as warranted by events.

---

[*] This is an edited, reformatted and augmented version of a Congressional Research Service Report RS22988, dated April 2, 2009.

Table 1. Iceland: Main Economic Indicators and Projections
(in billions of dollars and in percent)

	2004	2005	2006	2007	2008	2009
	Actual			Projected		
GDP(in $billions)	$9.9	$10.6	$11.1	$11.8	NA	NA
Real GDP growth	7.7%	7.4%	4.4%	4.9%	0.3%	−3.1%
CPI	3.2%	4.0%	6.8%	5.0%	12.1%	11.2%
Interest rates	7.5%	7.7%	9.3%	9.8%	11.4%	10.3%

Source: World Economic Outlook, October 2008, International Monetary Fund; and Economic Outlook, Preliminary Edition, June 2008, Organization for Economic Cooperation and Development.

BACKGROUND

Iceland is the smallest economy within the Organization for Economic Cooperation and Development (OECD) with a gross domestic product (GDP) in 2007 of about $11.8 billion, as indicated in **Table 1**. Historically, Iceland's economy has been based on marine and energy resources. More recently, Iceland has developed a strong services sector, which accounts for two-thirds of the economic output. Since 2000, Iceland has experienced particularly strong growth in its financial services sector. Trade accounts for a large share of Iceland's GDP, with imports and exports of goods and services equivalent in value to 46% and 35%, respectively, of GDP. Fish and other marine products were Iceland's main export item until 2006, when Iceland began to capitalize on its abundant thermal energy resources to produce and export aluminum. As the data in **Table 1** indicate, Iceland is expected to experience a slowdown in its rate of economic growth in 2008 and is projected by the International Monetary Fund to experience a negative rate of growth in 2009. Iceland also has battled a high and rising rate of inflation, as measured by the consumer price index (CPI) and interest rates, as measured by the long-term government bond rates.

RECENT ECONOMIC ACTIVITY

A combination of economic factors over the early to mid-2000s led to Iceland's current economic and banking distress. In particular, access to easy credit, a boom in domestic construction that fueled rapid economic growth, and a broad deregulation of Iceland's financial sector spurred the banks to expand rapidly abroad and eventually played a role in the eventual financial collapse. Iceland benefitted from favorable global financial conditions that reduced the cost of credit and a sweeping liberalization of its domestic financial sector that spurred rapid growth and encouraged Iceland's banks to spread quickly throughout Europe.

In 2004, Iceland's commercial banks increased their activity in the country's mortgage market by competing directly with the state-run Housing Financing Fund (HFF), which had been the major provider of mortgage loans. In contrast to the Housing Financing Fund, the commercial banks began offering loans with lower interest rates, longer maturities, and a higher loan to value ratio. Also, the banks did not require a real estate purchase as a precondition for a loan, which made it possible for homeowners to refinance existing mortgages and to access the equity in their homes for consumption or investment purposes. These measures spurred an expansion in credit and caused real estate prices to soar. In addition, the improving economic conditions led to an expansion in consumer spending which resulted in rising inflation and a larger trade deficit. As a further stimulus to the economy, the Icelandic government reduced both direct and indirect taxes, which provided further impetus to consumer spending.

By 2004, Iceland's central bank began tightening monetary policy by raising interest rates in an attempt to curtail inflationary pressures. Between 2004 and 2007, the Bank raised nominal short-term interest rates from 5% to 15%. The increase in interest rates, however, was not reflected in the interest rates the Housing Financing Fund charged for mortgages. As a result, the comparatively low interest rates charged by the HFF pushed up demand for housing which, in turn, further inflated the price of homes in Iceland. In addition, since the commercial banks were willing to make loans based on the equity in a home, the rising equity values in housing allowed consumers to finance a higher level of consumption, with the attendant pressure on inflation and interest rates. At the same time, the higher domestic interest rates made bond issues in krona attractive to foreign investors who could borrow abroad at low interest rates, which placed upward pressure on the value of the krona and worsened the trade deficit.

As Iceland deregulated its commercial banks, those banks expanded to the United Kingdom, the United States, Scandinavia, continental Europe, and elsewhere. Iceland has five commercial banks: Glitnir, Kaupthing, Nyi Landsbanki, Straumur Investment Bank, and Icebank, which serves as the clearing house for the 20 locally-run savings banks. The three largest banks, Kaupthing, Landsbanki, and Glitnir, have total assets of more than $168 billion, or 14 times Iceland's GDP. Iceland also has 20 savings banks, with assets at the end of 2007 valued at $9 billion.

After Iceland deregulated its commercial banks, the banks expanded their operations abroad by acquiring subsidiaries in commercial banking and in securities brokerages. At the end of 2007, almost half of the total assets of the largest commercial banking groups were accounted for by foreign subsidiaries, most of them located in Northern Europe, and in 2007 about 58% of their overall income was generated from their subsidiaries located abroad. By the end of 2007, Iceland's three largest banks relied on short-term financing for 75% of their funds, mostly through borrowing in the money markets and in the short-term interbank market. Iceland's banks are a hybrid between commercial and investment banks, with relatively large exposure to market risk. By March 2008, investors had become wary of Iceland's banks due to their large funding needs and high dependence on short-term funds in money markets. Even before the financial crisis erupted in fall 2008, the Central Bank of Iceland and other institutions forecasted a slowdown or a contraction in Iceland's rate of economic growth in 2008 and 2009.

BANKING COLLAPSE

In October 2008, Iceland's Financial Supervisory Authority (FSA), an independent state authority with responsibilities to regulate and supervise Iceland's credit, insurance, securities, and pension markets, took control of Iceland's three largest banks: Landsbanki, Glitnir Banki, and Kaupthing Bank. Subsequently, the FSA took over control of Iceland's last remaining large bank, Straumur Investment Bank, and it has reorganized the country's saving banks. On November 19, 2008, Iceland and the International Monetary Fund (IMF) finalized an agreement on an economic stabilization program supported by a $2.1 billion two-year standby arrangement from the IMF.[1] Upon approval of the IMF's Executive board, the IMF released $827 million immediately to Iceland with the remainder to be paid in eight equal installments, subject to quarterly reviews. Following the decision of IMF's Executive Board, Denmark, Finland, Norway, and Sweden agreed to provide an additional $2.5 billion in loans to Iceland. During this period, Iceland's central bank abandoned its attempt to maintain the value of the krona. With the take-over of the three major banks, the central bank effectively shut down the last clearing houses for trading krona.

As part of the IMF agreement, Iceland proposed a plan to restore confidence in its banking system, to stabilize the exchange rate, and to improve the nation's fiscal position. Also, as part of the plan, Iceland's central bank raised its key interest rate by six percentage points to 18% to attract foreign investors and to shore up its sagging currency.[2] The takeover of the banks was orchestrated in an attempt to quell a sharp depreciation in the exchange value of the Icelandic krona. The krona depreciated relative to the euro and the dollar between January 2008 and July 2008; the depreciation became more pronounced after July 2008. For Iceland, which relies heavily on trade, a sharp depreciation in its currency increases the costs of its imports and adds to domestic inflationary pressures.

On October 15, 2008, the Central Bank of Iceland set up a temporary system of daily currency auction to facilitate international trade. Without a viable currency, there was no way to support the banks, which have done the bulk of their business in foreign markets. The financial crisis also created problems with Great Britain, because hundreds of thousands of Britons hold accounts in online branches of the Icelandic banks and fear those accounts will all default. The government of British Prime Minister Gordon Brown used powers granted under anti-terrorism laws to freeze British assets of Landsbanki. Iceland filed suit in Britain to unfreeze the assets, but eventually dropped the suit.

The FSA moved to take over Iceland's major banks after Iceland's Parliament passed legislation that authorized the Treasury to disburse funds to the banks and that authorized the FSA to "take special measures" due to "special circumstances" in order to minimize harm or danger of harm to Iceland's financial markets.[3] The act authorizes Iceland's Treasury to contribute an amount up to 20% of the book value of the equity of the bank in return for shares in the bank that are equal in value to the capital contribution of the Treasury and for voting rights that are in proportion to the shares purchased through the Treasury funds. The measure also authorized the FSA to assume the powers of a shareholder's meeting, to suspend the Board of Directors, and to appoint a resolution committee to take over the assets, rights, and obligations of the troubled banks and to decide on any measures regarding the future of the three banks. The Financial Services Authority can limit or prohibit the disposal of the banks' capital or assets and can take custody of those assets that are required to meet the banks' obligations and can require that the assets be valued and disposed of for payments for claims.

One of the first acts of the three resolution committees was to guarantee the deposits that had been placed with the three banks. Next, the resolution committees established three new banking entities (New Landsbanki Islands HF, New Glitnir Banki, and New Kaupthing Bank) into which they placed the assets and a large share of the liabilities of the three existing banks. The foreign subsidiaries and foreign branches of the banks, however, remained with the old banks, except in those instances where the principal banking activities of the foreign branches were carried out in Iceland. In addition, certain other liabilities were not transferred to the new banks, including: securities issues and other borrowing; subordinated debt; income tax liabilities; and derivative contracts.

One issue that has been difficult to resolve has been determining the value of the assets and the liabilities that were transferred to the three new banks. According to the process established by the FSA, the value of the assets and liabilities of the three banks is being determined by a group of appraisers that was appointed by each of the resolution committees shortly after the three banks were reorganized. According to the IMF, that appraisal process has taken longer than initially expected and is now projected to be completed by early to mid-April 2009.[4] As part of the IMF's stand-by agreement, creditors agreed to delay the sale of any of the assets of the three banks, essentially placing a moratorium on payments to creditors. Creditors also have disagreed with the auditors over the value of the assets, which has delayed the time it is taking to restructure the old banks. Once that process is completed, a settlement will be arranged that will require the three new banks to pay the three old banks the "market value" of the assets and the liabilities at the time of the transfer of the assets and liabilities to the new banks. As a final stage in the process, the three new banks will be required to issue bonds to the old banks as payment for the assets. This process has been delayed further by creditors who have asked for more time to evaluate the structure of the bonds they will receive in compensation for the assets that were transferred to the new banks.

The demise of Iceland's three largest banks is attributed to an array of events, but primarily stems from decisions by the banks themselves. Some observers argued that the collapse of Lehman Brothers set in motion the events that finally led to the collapse of the banks,[5] but this conclusion is controversial. Some have argued that at the heart of Iceland's banking crisis is a flawed banking model that is based on an internationally active banking sector that is large relative to the size of the home country's GDP and to the fiscal capacity of the central bank.[6] As a result, a disruption in liquidity threatens the viability of the banks and overwhelms the ability of the central bank to act as the lender of last resort, which undermines the solvency of the banking system.

By the time of the acknowledged start of the global financial crisis in mid-2007, Iceland's central bank and Iceland's banks themselves had begun to recognize the vulnerability of the banks. In particular, officials in Iceland as well as financial observers in Europe had begun to reassess the risks associated with various financial instruments, and to raise questions about the asset strength of the banks and the asset size of the banks relative to the size of Iceland's economy. In addition, by late 2007, various organizations had begun to recognize the imbalances that were becoming apparent in Iceland's economy and had forecast a slowdown in Iceland's torrid pace of economic growth for 2008 and 2009.[7]

When Lehman Brothers collapsed, the international financial markets had already begun to reassess the risks associated with a broad range of financial instruments. Eventually, this reassessment of risks undermined the remaining amount of trust that existed in the credit markets, which caused banks and other financial firms to grow unwilling to make loans to short-term money markets and to engage in interbank lending, which caused those activities to freeze up. For Iceland's three largest banks, this collapse in short-term borrowing meant that they found that it was increasingly difficult to finance debts in the interbank market.

In addition, Iceland's Landsbanki and Kaupthing Bank experienced a sharp rise in the cost of private deposit insurance. This withdrawal of credit eliminated a major source of the bank's funding and threatened their ability to finance the nation's trade deficits. Typically, this situation is remedied by the central bank, which stands as the bank of last resort. In Iceland's case, however, the debts of the commercial banks were so large that Iceland's central bank was unable to guarantee the banks' loans, which lead to the collapse of the banks. In turn, the krona experienced a serious depreciation in its value, which raised the cost of imports and threatened to fuel domestic inflation. The large foreign debts held by Iceland's banks proved to be unsupportable once they could not utilize the interbank market to refinance their substantial loans.

CONCLUSIONS

The failure of Iceland's banks raises questions about bank supervision and crisis management for governments in Europe and the United States. This incident raises questions about how national governments should address the issue of supervising foreign financial firms that are operating within their borders and how to protect their depositors when a foreign-owned firm may attempt to withdraw deposits from one market in order to offset losses in another. One approach focuses on broad levels of cooperation between national governments with each government addressing the crisis from its own perspective and in its own limited way. For a number of governments in Europe this approach is appealing, because their economies and their banks have felt little direct effect from the crisis.

An alternative approach argues in favor of a more integrated and coordinated response from national governments and central banks. Proponents of this approach argue that a coordinated systemic approach is necessary, because financial markets in the United States and Europe have become highly integrated as a result of cross-border investment by banks, securities brokers, and other financial firms. As a result of this integration, economic and financial developments that affect national economies are difficult to contain and are quickly transmitted across national borders, as attested to by the financial crisis of 2008. As financial firms react to a financial crisis in one area, their actions can spill over to other areas as they withdraw assets from foreign markets to shore up their domestic operations. For instance, as Icelandic banks began to default, Britain used an anti-terrorism law to seize the deposits of the banks to prevent the banks from shifting funds from Britain to Iceland.[8] Banks and financial firms in Europe have felt the repercussions of the U.S. financial crisis as bank balance sheets have deteriorated and as U.S. firms and European firms have adjusted their operations in response to the crisis.

The Icelandic case also raises questions about the cost and benefits of branch banking across national borders where banks can grow to be so large that disruptions in the financial market can cause defaults that outstrip the resources of national central banks to address. Such branch banking across national borders has significantly expanded financial opportunities for individual investors and firms alike and is unlikely to disappear as a result of the current financial crisis. Nevertheless, if some financial institutions are deemed to be too big to fail, financial regulators and national governments may be called on to address the issue of how such institutions should be supervised when their operations span national borders and they are engaged in a vast array of banking and investment operations.

ACKNOWLEDGMENTS

This chapter relies heavily on *The Economy of Iceland*, The Central Bank of Iceland, August 2008.

End Notes

[1] Anderson, Camilla, Iceland Gets Help to Recover From Historic Crisis, *IMF Survey Magazine*, November 19, 2008.
[2] Iceland Raises Key Rate by 6 Percentage Points, *The New York Times*, October 29, 2008.
[3] Act No. 125/2008 on the Authority for Treasury Disbursements due to Unusual financial Market Circumstances etc., Prime Minister's Office, October 8, 2008.
[4] *Iceland: Stand-By Arrangement–Interim Review Under the Emergency Financing Mechanism*, International Monetary fund, February 2009,
[5] Portes, Richard, The Shocking Errors Behind Iceland's Meltdown, *Financial Times*, October 13, 2008, p. 15.
[6] Buiter, Willem H., and Anne Sibert, *The Icelandic Banking Crisis and What to Do About it: The Lender of Last Resort Theory of Optimal Currency Areas*. Policy Insight No. 26, Centre for Economic Policy Research, October 2008. p. 2.
[7] *The Economy of Iceland*, p. 9-11.
[8] Benoit, Bertrand, Tom Braithwaaite, Jimmy Burns, Jean Eaglesham, et al., Iceland and UK clash on Crisis, *Financial Times*, October 10, 2008, p. 1.

In: European Response to the Financial Crisis   ISBN: 978-1-60876-817-2
Editor: Baron L. Whitley   © 2010 Nova Science Publishers, Inc.

Chapter 5

THE U.S. FINANCIAL CRISIS: THE RESPONSE BY SWITZERLAND[*]

James K. Jackson

SUMMARY

As world financial and economic leaders met January 2009 in Davos, Switzerland for the annual World Economic Forum, Switzerland's renowned flagship banks were being battered by the financial crisis and the country was facing a potentially serious economic downturn. The current financial crisis has demonstrated that financial markets in Switzerland and elsewhere have become highly interdependent and that a crisis in one market can quickly spread to other markets across national borders.

For the United States, Switzerland is important as a member of international fora where the two countries share common interests while Swiss banks also act as competitors in the international financial marketplace. One issue the two countries share concerns the organization of financial markets domestically and abroad to improve supervision and regulation of individual institutions and of international markets. This issue also focuses on developing the organizational structures within national economies that can provide oversight of the different segments of the highly complex financial system.

Such oversight is viewed by many as critical, because financial markets are generally considered to play an indispensible role in allocating capital and facilitating economic activity.

In the months ahead, Members of Congress and the Obama administration likely will consider a number of proposals to restructure the supervisory and oversight responsibilities over the broad- based financial sector within the United States and in the broader international financial markets. The Swiss system provides an example of a system that has separated the regulatory and supervisory responsibilities from the monetary policy responsibilities of the Swiss National Bank and consolidated them into a national regulatory body that is subject to the Federal Council, or the executive of the Swiss government.

Overview

As world financial and economic leaders met January 2009 in Davos, Switzerland for the annual World Economic Forum, Switzerland's renowned flagship banks were being battered by the financial crisis and the country was facing a potentially serious economic downturn. The current financial crisis has demonstrated that financial markets in Switzerland and elsewhere have become highly interdependent and that a crisis in one market can quickly spread to other markets across national borders. As a result, Switzerland generally attempts to craft economic and financial policies in ways that preserve a careful balance between cooperation and competition with other financial centers in Europe and elsewhere. For the United States, Switzerland is important as a member of international fora where the two countries share common interests while Swiss banks also act as competitors in the international financial marketplace. The Swiss experience with resolution of troubled banks may provide a model for U.S. leaders to consider as they and other policymakers chart a course forward. In addition, Switzerland offers U.S. policymakers an alternative approach to consider in deciding how to regulate and supervise financial markets with the recent reorganization of its financial regulatory structure in a way that centralizes much of these responsibilities in a state body that is independent of Switzerland's central bank.

---

[*] This is an edited, reformatted and augmented version of a Congressional Research Service Report R40200, dated February 5, 2009.

In terms of the size of its Gross Domestic Product (GDP) Switzerland is one of the six largest advanced economies in Europe and is renowned as an important financial center. The Swiss people have chosen not to belong to the European Union,[1] so Switzerland maintains its own currency and charts independent monetary and exchange rate policies. Many in Switzerland initially viewed the financial crisis as a uniquely American phenomenon, but that view has changed as the Swiss government has had to approve a financial rescue package for the Union Bank of Switzerland (UBS), Switzerland's largest bank, and to move to amend national laws to improve depositor protection. Credit Suisse, Switzerland's second largest bank, so far has refused any funds from the government, but the bank has announced layoffs of more than 5,000 employees. UBS also has placed about $5 billion of its most illiquid loans and bonds into a separate funding facility that it will use to finance bonuses and compensation for its executives. In response to the financial crisis, the Swiss National Bank (SNB), similar to the U.S. Federal Reserve, has undertaken a series of cuts in key interest rates in cooperation with the European Central Bank and the U.S. Federal Reserve.

The recent experiences of Switzerland and other European countries (including Iceland, the United Kingdom, Sweden, and Austria) raise questions about how national governments can effectively supervise large financial firms that operate across national borders. This experience also raises questions about how governments can protect domestic depositors from financial troubles outside their national borders. The financial rescue for UBS also raises questions about the costs and benefits of branch banking across national borders where banks can grow to be so large that disruptions in the financial market can cause defaults that outstrip the resources of national central banks. Also, Switzerland's open economy has become highly intertwined with the broader European economy and its financial system has become highly integrated with the financial systems in Europe and elsewhere. As a result of this high degree of interdependence, the Swiss economy is quickly exposed to adverse economic and financial developments abroad, and it often experiences swings in economic activity that are greater than that experienced by other advanced economies.[2]

SWISS GOVERNMENT AND FINANCIAL SECTOR

Switzerland is governed by a Federal Council, a seven-member executive council which constitutes the federal government of Switzerland and serves as the Swiss collective head of state. As such, the Council approves major proposals to consider or to amend laws before the proposals are submitted to the Swiss Parliament. While the entire council is responsible for leading the federal administration of Switzerland, each Councilor heads one of the seven federal executive departments. The current members of the Federal Council are, in order of seniority:

- Moritz Leuenberger (SP), Federal Department of Environment, Transport, Energy and Communications
- Pascal Couchepin (FDP), Federal Department of Home Affairs
- Micheline Calmy-Rey (SP), Federal Department of Foreign Affairs
- Hans-Rudolf Merz (FDP), Federal Department of Finance, President of the Swiss Confederation for 2009
- Doris Leuthard (CVP), Federal Department of Economic Affairs, Vice-President of the Federal Council in 2009
- Eveline Widmer-Schlumpf (BDP).Federal Department of Justice and Police.
- Ueli Maurer (SVP), Federal Department of Defense, Civil Protection and Sports

The financial sector in Switzerland recently initiated a widespread restructuring that centralized the supervisory responsibilities over a broad swath of the financial sector into a regulatory body that is not directly controlled by Switzerland's central bank. Switzerland is not the only country to have such a regulatory structure. For instance, for member of the European Union (EU), supervisory responsibilities range from the central bank being the main supervisory authority with sector-specific institutions sharing some of the supervisory responsibilities to those in which there is a single supervisory authority independent from the central bank and those with a single supervisory authority with involvement by the central bank.[3] Although the Swiss restructuring was not triggered by the current financial crisis, it provides one possible model for other countries that are reconsidering their financial regulatory structure.

Within Switzerland, the financial sector is supervised by the Swiss National Bank (SNB), Switzerland's central bank, the Federal Department of Finance (similar to the U.S. Department of the Treasury) and the newly created Financial Management Authority (FINMA)[4] a state regulatory body which began operating January 1, 2009. In clear contrast with the U.S. regulatory structure, FINMA will assume regulatory responsibilities for a large part of the financial sector that is supervised in the United States by the Federal Reserve and the Securities and Exchange Commission. FINMA replaced the Swiss Federal Banking Commission in supervising banks, investment funds, stock exchanges, and securities trading, and the Federal Office of Private Insurance in supervising private insurance, health insurance, life insurance, and insurance brokers. FINMA also replaced the Anti-Money Laundering Control Authority and the Swiss Takeover Board. Under its director, Dr Patrick Raaflaub, FINMA is expected to employ some 320 staff members and spread over seven areas of activity (large banking groups, banks/financial intermediaries, integrated insurance supervision, insurance sectors, markets, legal, enforcement, international relations, and services). The strategic management of FINMA will be in the hands of its Board of Directors, chaired by Dr Eugen Haltiner.

The Swiss National Bank conducts traditional macroeconomic monetary policy with price stability, or a target rate of inflation below 2%, as its chief goal.[5] It implements its monetary policy by targeting the three-month LIBOR rate, rather than the more traditional overnight interbank lending rate, in order to influence money market interest rates. Similar to the U.S. system, the Swiss banking system operates on a reserve basis, where commercial banks are required to satisfy minimum reserve requirements, currently 2.5%, of a bank's short-term liabilities.

The Swiss financial sector, known for its long-standing experience in asset management, performs an important international intermediation function within the global financial system as one of the key players in the international private banking business.[6] Within the Swiss economy, financial services play a large role, accounting for about 12% of GDP and employing about 200,000 people.[7] As **Table 1** indicates, the Swiss financial system is highly developed and diversified. It consists of about 330 banks, a small number of global players in banking and insurance, a large and diversified insurance sector, many pension funds, and two dozen cantonal (state) banks. UBS and Credit Suisse, Switzerland's two largest banks, are complex financial institutions that operate globally and offer a broad range of products and services. The cantonal banks are owned in part or in whole by the cantons, which typically guarantee their liabilities. Regional banks engage exclusively in domestic banking. Raiffeisen banks consist of over 500 credit cooperatives and focus on mortgages in rural areas. The private banks engage primarily in portfolio management for high net worth individuals, and the foreign banks represent subsidiaries of foreign banks that also generally focus on private banking.

Table 1. Switzerland's Financial Sector, Number of Firms by Market

	2005	2006	2007
All	337	331	330
Cantonal banks	24	24	24
Large banks	2	2	2
Regional and savings banks	79	78	76
Raiffeisen banks	1	1	1
Other banks	189	183	183
Commercial banks	7	7	7
Stock exchange banks	56	52	48
Other banks	4	4	6
Foreign controlled banks	122	120	122
Branches of foreign banks	28	29	30
Private bankers	14	14	14
Insurance companies – life	24	24	24
Insurance companies – general	124	124	124

Source:Swiss National Bank

Switzerland takes an active part in such international organizations as the International Monetary Fund (IMF), the G-10 group of industrialized countries[8], the G-20, the Bank for International Settlements (BIS)[9], the Organization for Economic Cooperation and Development (OECD)[10], the World Trade Organization (WTO), the Financial Stability Forum (FSF)[11], and the United Nations. In addition, Switzerland has been a member of the Financial Action Task Force (FATF)[12] since 1990 and was instrumental in proposing stricter guidelines in 2003 concerning identifying clients and the ultimate beneficial owner of bank accounts.[13]

Recent estimates indicate that Switzerland had a Gross Domestic Product (GDP) in 2008 of about $500 billion and a per capita income of slightly over $42,000, as indicated in **Table 2**. The current financial crisis is taking a toll on the Swiss economy, which is forecast to slow down sharply in 2009, with recovery not expected to come until 2010.[14]

Table 2. Switzerland, Key Economic Indicators

	2007	2008	2009	2010
Nominal GDP ($billions)	426.7	493.4	470.2	473.6
Real GDP growth (%)	3.3	1.8	−1.8	0.3
Population (millions)	7.6	7.7	7.7	7.8
GDP per capita ($)	40,320	42,123	41,736	41,837
Unemployment rate (%)	2.8	2.6	4.1	5.4
General government balance (%of GDP)	2.2	0.9	−1.7	−2.6
Consumer prices (% change)	0.7	2.4	−0.2	0.9
Money market rate (%)	2.5	2.6	0.2	0.3
Current account balance ($billion)	58.0	42.0	37.3	34.8

Source: Switzerland, Country Report, Economist Intelligence Unit, January 2009.
Note: Data for 2009 and 2010 are estimates.

SWITZERLAND AND THE FINANCIAL CRISIS

Switzerland's efforts to contain the negative effects of the financial crisis initially seemed to be effective,[15] but the spreading crisis and the associated economic downturn are taking a toll on the Swiss economy. The cause and effects of the current financial crisis likely will be debated for years to come. This memorandum does not attempt to provide a complete explanation of the causes of the financial crisis, since other CRS Reports provide such a detailed explanation.[16] While different individuals and organizations will view the crisis from different perspectives, a rough way to view the crisis is as a series of events proceeding through four periods where the policy responses differed.[17] The periods are not necessarily discretely identifiable because they overlap with other periods, but this approach provides a short-hand way of describing the crisis and explaining Switzerland's actions.

Phase I: Build-up

In general terms, the financial crisis can be thought of as beginning in August 2007, although the seeds of the crisis likely had been in place for some time. The crisis is identified with a loss of confidence in credit markets that was associated with a downturn in the U.S. sub-prime mortgage market. While a downturn in mortgage markets generally would be expected to have a negative impact on parts of the economy, the crisis quickly evolved into a more general liquidity crunch that spread well beyond the sub-prime mortgage market. Initially, this first period of the crisis appeared to affect highly leveraged banks, investment firms, and other financial services providers, which prompted an ad hoc case-by case response. For instance, the Federal Deposit Insurance Corporation took control of IndyMac Bank, the Federal Reserve arranged for JPMorgan Chase to acquire Bear Sterns, and the British government nationalized housing lender Northern Rock.

Phase II: Liquidity Issues

In the second period, as U.S. mortgage markets continued to deteriorate, the U.S. Treasury announced that it was taking over the Federal National Mortgage Association (Fannie Mae) and the Federal Home Loan Mortgage Corporation (Freddie Mac).. Soon after this takeover, Lehman Brothers filed for bankruptcy, which led to a more wide-spread crisis of confidence. This lack of confidence, in turn, was a major factor in causing credit markets to freeze up and it led to a lack of liquidity. In this period, the policy emphasis shifted from rescuing individual banks and institutions to responding to the broader systemic issues that were affecting a wide range of credit markets. The Federal Reserve provided financial assistance to American International Group (AIG) and approved the transformation of Goldman Sachs and Morgan Stanley into bank holding companies. On October 8, 2008, the Federal Reserve, the European Central Bank, the Bank of England and the central banks of Canada, Sweden, Switzerland, the Bank of Japan, and the Chinese central Bank all lowered their lending rates to reduce borrowing costs and to provide liquidity Before the end of the month, the Federal Reserve announced another cut in interest rates, which other central banks followed in November. In addition, various central banks increased guarantees to depositors holders. The International Monetary Fund (IMF) approved a short-term liquidity facility to assist banks facing liquidity problems.

Phase III: Solvency Issues

In the third phase, the lack of confidence in credit markets and a lack of liquidity also sparked concerns over the adequacy of capital provisions of financial institutions and to concerns over the solvency of banks and other financial institutions. During this phase, financial firms attempted to deleverage by reducing the amount of troubled assets on their balance sheets. At the same time, the stocks of most financial firms dropped markedly and the value of their assets continued to decline, which weakened an even larger number of institutions. In this phase, intervention by central banks continued, but national governments also began to intervene, typically through their respective Treasury departments, to take control of insolvent banks or otherwise to provide financial assistance. The U.S. Congress passed the Troubled Assets Relief Program (P.L. 110-343), and the U.K. government provided assistance to the Royal Bank of Scotland, Lloyds TSB, and to Hallifax Bank of Scotland (HBOS). Several European countries, including Germany, France, Italy, Austria, Netherlands, Portugal, Spain, and Norway announced plans to recapitalize banks and to provide government debt guarantees. At a meeting of the G-20, leaders agreed to take steps to stabilize the global financial system.

Phase IV: Fiscal Intervention

In the fourth period, as the problems in credit markets persisted, the financial crisis spread to those activities in the real economy that are highly reliant on credit markets and it reinforced concerns over the adequacy of capital provisions. Furthermore, the slowdown in economic growth weakened the capital position of financial institutions so that the financial crisis and the economic downturn have become negatively reinforcing. Governments have responded in this phase of the crisis by adopting macroeconomic stimulus measures to blunt the effects of the economic recession in addition to providing liquidity, guaranteeing the safety of deposits, and providing funds to improve the capital position of banks and other financial institutions. In February 2008, the U.S. Congress passed P.L. 110-185, the Economic Stimulus Act of 2008 to provide rebates to individual on their income taxes in order to provide a fiscal boost to the U.S. economy.[18] Then in July 2008, the U.S. Congress adopted, and President Bush signed, P.L. 110-289, the Housing and Economic Recovery Act of 2008 to provide an additional fiscal stimulus to the U.S. economy. In February 2009, the Congress is considering H.R. 1 and S. 1, the American Recovery and Reinvestment Act of 2009[19] to provide an additional fiscal stimulus to the U.S. economy. The U.K. government announced a fiscal stimulus package and the EU governments approved a economic stimulus package for its members. in addition, the U.K. government and the German governments have announced additional stimulus packages. Various central banks also announced additional cuts in key interest rates as another measure to stimulate economic growth.

Switzerland's Response

Switzerland has chosen to address the financial crisis in it own distinct way. It has not followed Iceland,[20] which essentially nationalized its troubled banks, or Sweden,[21] which nearly a decade earlier had restructured its troubled banks by creating a separate entity to work out failing loans. As a first step, the Swiss National Bank moved to address concerns over liquidity by engaging in coordinated actions with other leading central banks. It lowered key interest rates on October 8, 2008, November 7, 2008, November 20, 2008, and on December 8, 2008, bringing the key interest rate to 0.5% in December 2008. In addition, in September 2008, the SNB addressed concerns over the capital adequacy of its two largest banks by contributing $15 billion to a $100 billion emergency injection of liquidity. Also in September 2008, the Swiss Government introduced a 900 million Swiss franc-package of measures to stimulate the Swiss economy. Then, in December, 2008, Swiss Economic Minister Doris Leuthard announced that the Swiss government had development a second economic stimulus package that was worth about 650 million Swiss francs-mostly in infrastructure projects to be implemented in 2009, out of concerns that the Swiss economy was headed for its worst recession in nearly 20 years. Reportedly, the Swiss Cabinet is preparing a third package of economic stimulus measures for 2010 should economic conditions in Switzerland continue to deteriorate.

Also, to improve the capital adequacy of Switzerland's largest bank, Switzerland's Federal Council formally adopted on November 5, 2008 a package of measures proposed by the Federal Council, the Swiss National Bank and the Swiss Federal Banking Commission (now FINMA) to stabilize the Swiss financial system. The Dispatch adopted by the Council provided $60 billion in aid to UBS and a draft of measures to be submitted to parliament to amend Switzerland's Federal Act on Banks and Savings Banks (Banking Act) to strengthen depositor protection.

The Swiss package of measures are aimed both at relieving UBS of illiquid assets and at strengthening the bank's equity capital. UBS, and to a lesser extent Credit Suisse, was exposed in the credit default swap market,[22] and it had a particularly high exposure to U.S. subprime assets that required UBS to write down the value of a substantial part of its portfolio.[23] In addition to these problems in the banking sector, the International Monetary Fund (IMF) concluded in a recent review of Switzerland's economy that the country's insurers derive a large share of their income from overseas business and, therefore they would experience the effects from a slowdown in economic activity both within and outside of Switzerland.[24]

The first part of the Swiss financial package is intended to provide liquid assets through two actions. First is the transfer of up to $60 billion of currently illiquid UBS assets to a special entity that would be operated and overseen by the Swiss National Bank to bring additional liquidity to UBS, while relieving it of risks. UBS is expected to provide this fund with equity capital of up to $6 billion. With a secure loan to fund the new entity, the SNB is then expected to finance up to $54 billion in loans, not with its own capital, but by raising U.S. dollars initially with the U.S. Federal Reserve and later directly in the market. The fund entity is to charge interest commensurate with the risks and is to compensate the SNB for the risks involved.

As collateral, the SNB is to have ownership of the assets and control of the fund entity, as well as the overwhelming share of the equity in the event of positive performance. The assets transferred from UBS consist primarily of loans associated with U.S. and European residential and commercial real estate mortgages. The underwriting price reportedly is to be determined on the basis of the current book value of the assets and on the basis of an independent evaluation. The entity is to pay the lower of the two prices. The transfer of assets to the fund entity and the administration and liquidation of the assets is to be supervised by the SNB.

In the second measure, the capital base of UBS is to be reinforced by the Swiss government subscribing to 6 billion Swiss francs of mandatory convertible notes. This measure is directly connected to relieving UBS of illiquid assets by allowing the bank to fund an entity with the necessary capital, without diminishing its own capital base. For the Swiss government the mandatory convertible notes offer the expectation that the notes are secure and that the government will be commensurately compensated (coupons of 12.5 %) and that the government will not, at least not initially, become a co-owner of the bank. The Federal Council has indicated that it is committed to putting a time limit on the participation of the government.

In addition to the measures to assist UBS, the Federal Council instructed the FDF to improve the Swiss depositor protection system. As an immediate measure, the Federal Council indicated that it would submit a Dispatch to parliament in the winter session of 2009 to increase depositor protection from 30,000 Swiss francs to 100,000 francs and to increase the system limits from 4 billion francs to 6 billion francs. In a second phase, the Council indicated that it intends to revise completely the current deposit guarantee scheme. The Federal Council has indicated that it expects to see a reform proposal from the FDF by the end of March 2009. The emergency provisions are intended to remain in force until December 31, 2010. By then it is expected that the improved depositor protection proposal will be integrated into standard law.

In addition to the measures outlined above, the Swiss proposal is intended to strengthen the financial system through four other measures:

1. First, current reforms to company law are expected to be amended by adding regulations on executive compensation. At the same time FINMA is expected to draw up minimum standards for the entire financial sector. In addition and after prior consultation with FINMA, UBS will be obliged to submit its compensation for its board of directors and management in line with established international institutions. The involvement of the government after that will be subject to the condition that UBS implements the requirements of the Federal Council in the area of corporate governance. A report on implementation will be provided as part of the Federal Council business report and the federal accounts.
2. Second, by November 2008, the SFBC was required to issue more stringent capital requirements for major banks.
3. Third, by the spring of 2009, the Federal Council intends to conduct a fundamental review of the deposit guarantee system.
4. Finally the Federal Council indicated that it would remain prepared, if necessary, to guarantee new medium-term bank borrowings of Swiss banks in the capital market.

As a final measure, the Federal Council intends to introduce an additional capital buffer to increase the target value for supplementary capital requirements above those of Basel II[25], which the Swiss government hopes will better cover the systemic risks of the big banks. This further tightening of the capital requirements should go beyond the existing Swiss requirements and the planned tightening of conditions of the Basel Committee. FINMA also intends to introduce a leverage ratio. This would act as a buffer against losses resulting from a false assessment of risks and which are not adequately covered by the requirements of Basel II.

The importance of Switzerland's efforts to support UBS and Credit Suisse is clear from the data in **Table 3**. The foreign exposure of Switzerland's banks, in terms of the stock of foreign assets, grew to exceed the size of Switzerland's GDP, which challenges the ability of national central banks to act as a lender of last resort. Often, banks' foreign exposure is analyzed as a way of assessing risks to the financial system and as an early warning of developments that could stress the system. Over 70% of this exposure, both in terms of claims and liabilities, is in interbank activity. As **Table 3** indicates, UBS had assets in 2008 that were nearly five times the size of Switzerland's economy, while Credit Suisse had assets that were three times the size of the Swiss economy.

Table 3. Size of Selected European Banks

Country	Bank Name	Total Assets (billions of euros)	Total Assets to GDP (percent of GDP)
Iceland	Kaupthing	53	623
Switzerland	UBS	1,426	484
Iceland	Landsbanki	32	374
Switzerland	Credit Suisse	854	854
Netherlands	ING	1,370	290
Belgium &Lux.	Fortis	886	254
Cyprus	Bank of Cyprus	32	253
Belgium &Lux.	Dexia	605	173
Spain	Santander	913	132
United Kingdom	RBS	2,079	126
Netherlands	Rabobank	571	121
France	BNP Parabas	1,694	104
Ireland	Bank of Ireland	183	102
Belgium &Lux.	KBC	356	102

Source: O'Murchu,Cynthia,and Emma Saunders,Are European Banks Too Big to Fail?,Financial Times, September 30,2008.

CONCLUSION

The U.S. and Swiss economies and financial systems are markedly different in size and scope. Each country is facing its own set of circumstances and challenges as a result of the financial crisis. These two countries, however, often cooperate in a number of international organizations, while the international scope of their financial activities often cause firms operating in their respective regulatory jurisdictions to compete. One issue the two countries share concerns the organization of financial markets domestically and abroad to improve supervision and regulation of individual institutions and of international markets. This issue also focuses on developing the organizational structures within national economies that can provide oversight of the different segments of the highly complex financial system. Such oversight is viewed by many as critical, because financial markets are generally considered to play an indispensible role in allocating capital and facilitating economic activity. The financial crisis also has revealed extensive interdependency across financial market segments both within many of the advanced national financial markets and across national borders. Some observers have argued that the complexity of the financial system has outstripped the ability of national regulators to oversee effectively.

In the months ahead, Members of Congress and the Obama administration likely will consider a number of proposals to restructure the supervisory and oversight responsibilities over the broad- based financial sector within the United States and in the broader international financial markets. As policymakers address this issue, they likely will assess the costs and benefits of centralizing supervisory responsibilities into a few key entities, such as the Federal Reserve, or dispersed them more widely across a number of different entities. In the United States, the Federal Reserve holds a monopoly over the conduct of monetary policy, mainly as a means of keeping such policy-making independent from political pressure, but has shared regulatory and supervisory responsibilities with a number of different agencies that are more directly accountable to elected officials and are subject to change. The Swiss system provides an example of a system that has separated the regulatory and supervisory responsibilities from the monetary policy responsibilities of the Swiss National Bank and consolidated them into a national regulatory body that is subject to the Federal Council, or the executive of the Swiss government. Since this newly created entity began operating on January 1, 2009, it is still too early to assess the effectiveness of this system, but it may merit watching closely as a possible alternative to the existing U.S. structure.

End Notes

[1] Members of the European Union are: Austria, Belgium, Bulgaria, Cyprus, the Czech Republic, Denmark, Estonia, Finland, France, Germany, Greece, Hungary, Republic of Ireland, Italy, Latvia, Lithuania, Luxembourg, Malta, the Netherlands, Poland, Portugal, Romania, Slovakia, Slovenia, Sweden, and the United Kingdom.

[2] *Switzerland: 2008 Article IV Consultation*, International Monetary Fund, IMF Country Report No. 08/170. May 2008. International Monetary Fund.

[3] Hardy, Daniel, A "European Mandate" for Financial Sector Authorities in the EU, in *Euro Area Policies: Selected Issues*, International Monetary Fund, IMF Country Report No. 08/263, August 2008.

[4] *About FINMA*, FINMA.

[5] *The Swiss National Bank in Brief*, Swiss National Bank, August 2007.

[6] *Switzerland: 2008 Article IV Consultation*, p. 3.

[7] *Figures on Switzerland as a Location for Financial Services*, Federal Department of Finance, December 2008.

[8] The G-10 group includes Belgium, Canada, France, Germany, Italy, Japan, Netherlands, Sweden, Switzerland, the United Kingdom, and the United States.

[9] The Bank for International Settlements is an international banking organization that was organized in 1930 to foster international monetary and financial cooperation and serves as a bank for central banks. The bank sponsors meetings if central bankers and collects data from central banks and publishes reports and data on the international flows of capital between financial centers. BIS provides a wide range of financial services to central banks to assist them in managing their foreign exchange reserves, extends short-term credits to central banks, and has on occasion extended short-term credits to countries facing financial troubles

[10] The Organization for Economic Cooperation and Development is an international group of 30 advanced economies that provides a structure where governments can compare policy experiences, seek answers to common problems, identify good practices, and coordinate domestic and international policies The member countries include Australia, Austria, Belgium, Canada, the Czech Republic, Denmark, Finland, France, Germany, Greece, Hungary, Iceland, Ireland, Italy, Japan, Korea, Luxembourg, Mexico, The Netherlands, New Zealand, Norway, Poland, Portugal, Slovak Republic, Spain, Sweden, Switzerland, Turkey, United Kingdom, and the United States.

[11] The financial Stability Forum is an international organization that brings together senior representatives of national financial authorities (central banks, supervisory authorities and treasury departments), international financial institutions, international regulatory and supervisory groupings, committees of central bank experts and the European Central Bank. The FSF is serviced by a small secretariat housed at the Bank for International Settlements in Basel, Switzerland.

[12] The Financial Action Task Force on Money Laundering is comprised of 31 member countries and territories and two international organizations. It was organized to develop and promote policies to combat money laundering and terrorist financing. CRS Report RS2 1904, *The Financial Action Task Force: An Overview*, by James K. Jackson.

[13] *Swiss Financial Centre and Financial Market Policy*, Federal Department of Finance.

[14] *Switzerland, Country Report*, Economist Intelligence Unit, January 2009; and *OECD Economic Outlook*, Switzerland, the Organization for Economic Cooperation and Development.

[15] For information see CRS Report RL34742, *The U.S. Financial Crisis: The Global Dimension with Implications for U.S. Policy*, coordinated by Dick K. Nanto.

[16] See CRS Report RL34182, *Financial Crisis? The Liquidity Crunch of August 2007*, by Darryl E. Getter et al.; CRS Report R40007, *Financial Market Turmoil and U.S. Macroeconomic*

Performance, by Craig K. Elwell; CRS Report RL34412, *Containing Financial Crisis*, by Mark Jickling; CRS Report RS22963, *Financial Market Intervention*, by Edward V. Murphy and Baird Webel; and CRS Report RL34742, *The U.S. Financial Crisis: The Global Dimension with Implications for U.S. Policy*, coordinated by Dick K. Nanto.

[17] Fender, Ingo, and Jacob Gyntelberg, Overview: Global Financial Crisis Spurs Unprecedented Policy Actions, *BIS Quarterly Review*, Bank for International Settlements, December 2008.

[18] CRS Report RS22850, *Tax Provisions of the 2008 Economic Stimulus Package*, coordinated by Jane G. Gravelle.

[19] CRS Report R40104, *Economic Stimulus: Issues and Policies*, by Jane G. Gravelle, Thomas L. Hungerford, and Marc Labonte.

[20] CRS Report RS22988, *Iceland's Financial Crisis*, by James K. Jackson.

[21] CRS Report RS22962, *The U.S. Financial Crisis: Lessons From Sweden*, by James K. Jackson.

[22] Credit default swaps are insurance-like contracts that promise to cover losses on certain securities in the event of a default or other credit event. They typically apply to municipal bonds, corporate debt and mortgage securities and are sold by banks, hedge funds and others. The buyer of the credit default insurance pays premiums over a period of time in return for peace of mind, knowing that losses will be covered if a default happens. They are supposed to work similarly to someone taking out home insurance to protect against losses from fire and theft.

[23] *Switzerland: 2008 Article IV Consultation*, p. 8.

[24] Ibid., p. 17.

[25] Basel II is the second of the Basel Accords, which are recommendations on banking laws and regulations issued by the Basel Committee on Banking Supervision. The purpose of Basel II is to create an international standard that banking regulators can use when creating regulations concerning requirements for capital adequacy that banks must meet to guard against the types of financial and operational risks that banks face.

INDEX

A

accountability, 40, 56, 58
accounting, 57, 59, 107
accounting standards, 57
acquisitions, 43, 75
adaptation, 18
administration, ix, 31, 75, 104, 106, 113, 116
advisory body, 79
aggregate demand, 19
aid, 23, 33, 38, 62, 66, 67, 91, 112
alternative, 53, 70, 100, 104, 116
amendments, 24
analysts, viii, 85, 86, 91
annual rate, 44
anti-terrorism, 71, 97, 100
assessment, 55, 115
assets, viii, 38, 45, 46, 47, 48, 52, 54, 56, 59, 71, 75, 81, 85, 86, 89, 90, 96, 97, 98, 100, 111, 113, 115
auditing, 70
Australia, 82, 117
Austria, vii, 41, 47, 58, 64, 79, 105, 111, 117
authority, viii, 70, 80, 85, 96, 106
automatic stabilisers, 16

B

balance sheet, viii, 48, 56, 81, 85, 86, 87, 90, 100, 111
Balkans, 30
bank account, 43, 108
bank failure, 48, 91
Bank of America, 82
Bank of Canada, 82
Bank of England, 51, 53, 55, 60, 80, 81, 82, 84, 110
Bank of Japan, 82, 110
Bank of Korea, 82
bankers, 108, 117
banking, vii, viii, ix, 15, 22, 40, 43, 48, 50, 51, 57, 58, 67, 69, 71, 73, 74, 84, 85, 86, 87, 89, 90, 93, 95, 96, 97, 98, 99, 100, 105, 107, 113, 117, 118
Banking Committee, 73
banking industry, 51
bankruptcy, 49, 88, 110
barrier, 76
barriers, 76, 80
Basel Committee, 84, 115, 118
Basel II, 77, 84, 114, 118
basis points, 51
Belarus, 38, 41
Belgium, 41, 47, 62, 64, 79, 115, 117
benefits, 12, 20, 24, 30, 32, 39, 61, 62, 63, 66, 71, 72, 79, 80, 100, 105, 116

Bernanke, Ben, 81
binding, 79, 80
BIS, 48, 58, 81, 108, 117, 118
boilers, 24
bonds, 51, 81, 86, 98, 105, 118
bonus, 61
borrowers, 15, 58, 89, 91
borrowing, 54, 87, 96, 98, 99, 110
Bosnia, 38
branching, 75
Brazil, 31, 82
Britain, 67, 71, 83, 97, 100
broadband, 24, 27
budget deficit, 80, 83
budgetary resources, 17
building societies, 51
buildings, 24, 27, 62, 63, 67
Bulgaria, 41, 79, 117
buyer, 81, 118
bypass, 79

C

Canada, 31, 45, 53, 82, 110, 117
CAP, 24
capital flows, 70
carbon, 13, 24, 31, 61
carmakers, 61
case study, viii, 85
cash flow, 23
catalyst, 13, 20
categorization, 77
Central Europe, 38
certificates of deposit, 87
certification, 24
China, 31, 53, 82
circulation, 27
citizens, 14, 15, 21
clean energy, 42, 60, 61
clients, 67, 77, 108
climate change, 13, 18, 24, 31, 32
Co, 39, 65, 83, 94, 108, 117
CO2, 27
collateral, 50, 51, 81, 113
commercial bank, 51, 95, 96, 99, 107

Committee on Intelligence, 79
commodity, 46
compensation, 98, 105, 114
competition, 15, 22, 31, 33, 43, 55, 104
competitive advantage, 59
competitiveness, 13, 19, 20, 57
competitors, ix, 103, 104
complement, 42
complexity, 46, 69, 116
compliance, 30, 33, 43, 79
compounds, 59
concentration, 75, 76
confidence, vii, 11, 13, 15, 16, 20, 29, 30, 32, 46, 49, 90, 97, 109, 110
Congress, ix, 35, 36, 39, 56, 60, 104, 111, 116
consensus, 40, 69, 88
consolidation, 30
constraints, 23, 57
construction, vii, 11, 24, 27, 61, 62, 63, 67, 88, 95
consumer price index, 94
consumers, 17, 24, 30, 46, 66, 95
consumption, vii, 11, 17, 18, 24, 27, 33, 64, 65, 66, 95
contracts, 49, 81, 98, 118
control, 47, 56, 86, 96, 110, 111, 113
convergence, 19, 73, 79
Copenhagen, 31
corporate governance, 114
corporate restructuring, 76
corporations, 23, 81
costs, 23, 24, 39, 43, 46, 72, 97, 105, 110, 116
Council of the European Union, 73
CPI, 94
credibility, 68, 90, 91
credit, vii, ix, 11, 14, 17, 18, 37, 45, 46, 49, 52, 54, 56, 57, 60, 62, 66, 67, 68, 70, 74, 78, 81, 85, 86, 87, 90, 91, 95, 96, 99, 108, 109, 110, 111, 113, 118
credit market, 37, 45, 46, 49, 54, 56, 60, 74, 99, 109, 110, 111
credit rating, 57, 70
creditors, 91, 98

creditworthiness, 91
crisis management, 100
cross-border, 29, 43, 60, 61, 71, 75, 76, 100
cross-border investment, 71, 100
cross-country, 54
CRS, 35, 44, 80, 81, 83, 86, 93, 104, 109, 117, 118
currency, 48, 53, 54, 68, 73, 74, 79, 87, 90, 97, 105
current account, 87
current account deficit, 87
Cyprus, 79, 115, 117
Czech Republic, 40, 64, 79, 117

D

danger, 12, 97
debt, viii, 47, 49, 51, 52, 55, 58, 68, 70, 80, 81, 85, 87, 98, 111, 118
debts, 52, 89, 99
decision makers, 90
decision making, 78
decisions, ix, 27, 73, 78, 80, 82, 93, 98
deduction, 62
defense, 63
deficit, 18, 66, 68
deficits, 19, 38, 72, 80, 86, 87, 99
democracy, 79
Denmark, ix, 47, 49, 54, 64, 65, 79, 82, 93, 97, 117
Department of Defense, 106
Department of Justice, 106
deposits, 70, 71, 98, 100, 111
depreciation, 38, 97, 99
deregulation, 86, 87, 95
derivatives, 52
desalination, 62
destruction, 27
developed countries, 29, 31, 53
developing countries, 29, 31
Development Assistance, 31
development banks, 24
development policy, 73
direct investment, 87
directives, 73, 75, 76

disaster, 63
discipline, viii, 18, 78, 80, 82, 85, 91
disclosure, 77
discretionary, 17
dispersion, 39
distress, 95
division, 67
Doha, 30, 31
domestic credit, ix, 87, 93
domestic demand, viii, 35, 55, 57, 90
domestic investment, 87
domestic laws, 75, 76
donor, 31
donors, 32
downsized, 12
draft, 58, 112
duration, 17

E

early warning, 41, 115
Eastern Europe, viii, 35, 38, 40, 41, 70, 80
ECOFIN, 73
economic activity, vii, ix, 17, 36, 39, 46, 69, 72, 104, 105, 113, 116
Economic and Monetary Union, 80, 82
economic crisis, 19, 32, 37, 38, 70, 71
economic downturn, viii, ix, 13, 29, 35, 37, 38, 39, 43, 44, 45, 46, 56, 59, 60, 66, 69, 74, 103, 104, 109, 111
economic fundamentals, 19
economic growth, 36, 37, 38, 40, 44, 46, 55, 57, 60, 63, 71, 72, 80, 87, 89, 90, 94, 95, 96, 99, 111
economic growth rate, 63
economic integration, viii, 36, 70, 73
economic performance, 30
economic policy, 13, 73
economic problem, 40, 86
economic resources, 36
economic union, 72
education, 27
effective exchange rate, 88
electric power, 24
electricity, 24

emerging economies, 12, 29, 58, 70
emission, 27
employability, 21
employees, 66, 105
employers, 18, 21, 62
employment, 16, 20, 21, 27, 57, 63, 80
EMU, 80, 82
energy, 13, 18, 20, 22, 23, 24, 27, 31, 32, 33, 57, 60, 61, 62, 63, 68, 80, 94
energy consumption, 27, 33
energy efficiency, 18, 22, 23, 24, 61, 63, 68
engagement, 29
England, 55, 60, 81, 82
entrepreneurs, 21, 23
entrepreneurship, 22, 23
environment, 18, 43, 76, 80
environmental protection, 23, 33
environmental standards, 23
equities, 46
equity, 15, 24, 43, 49, 53, 68, 77, 88, 89, 95, 97, 113
equity market, 43
Estonia, 41, 79, 117
Euro, 38, 45, 48, 55, 67, 79, 80, 81, 82, 117
Europe, viii, 12, 13, 16, 21, 24, 27, 30, 32, 36, 37, 38, 39, 43, 44, 46, 48, 52, 53, 54, 56, 66, 69, 70, 71, 72, 76, 79, 80, 81, 82, 83, 84, 88, 89, 95, 96, 99, 100, 104, 105
European Central Bank, viii, 12, 15, 35, 40, 42, 43, 46, 50, 51, 53, 54, 57, 59, 60, 73, 74, 80, 81, 82, 83, 105, 110, 117
European Commission, 32, 42, 52, 56, 60, 73, 74, 78, 80, 82
European Community, 43, 80, 82
European Court of Justice, 73
European Investment Bank, 15, 38
European Monetary Union, 82
European Parliament, 31, 32, 73, 78, 79
European Social Fund, 21, 58, 83
Eurostat, 80
exchange controls, 87
exchange rate, viii, 12, 63, 85, 86, 87, 90, 97, 105
exchange rate policy, 86, 87
exchange rates, 63

execution, viii, 77, 85
expenditures, 46
exports, 12, 37, 55, 68, 72, 94
exposure, 38, 41, 43, 46, 49, 96, 113, 115

F

failure, 70, 100
Fannie Mae, 49, 110
FDP, 106
Federal Deposit Insurance Corporation, 47, 110
federal government, 36, 106
Federal Reserve, 39, 48, 49, 50, 51, 53, 54, 60, 81, 91, 105, 107, 110, 113, 116
Federal Reserve Bank, 91
finance, 21, 22, 23, 27, 45, 54, 57, 67, 73, 74, 81, 87, 95, 99, 105, 113
financial development, 71, 100, 105
financial institution, 32, 36, 37, 38, 40, 42, 45, 51, 52, 54, 56, 60, 71, 100, 107, 111, 117
financial institutions, 36, 37, 38, 42, 45, 51, 52, 54, 56, 60, 71, 100, 107, 111
financial intermediaries, 107
financial markets, ix, 15, 29, 36, 37, 39, 40, 41, 46, 48, 49, 50, 52, 69, 70, 71, 74, 76, 80, 87, 93, 97, 99, 100, 103, 104, 116
financial oversight, 52
financial regulation, 75, 78
financial resources, 27, 78
financial sector, ix, 15, 39, 46, 52, 58, 70, 73, 75, 86, 90, 95, 104, 106, 107, 114, 116
Financial Services Action Plan (FSAP) 43, 72, 75, 80, 84
Financial Services Authority, 50, 84, 98
financial stability, 42, 74
financial support, 15, 22, 39, 51, 91
financial system, vii, ix, 36, 38, 39, 41, 45, 50, 55, 57, 58, 69, 74, 86, 91, 103, 105, 107, 111, 112, 114, 115, 116
financing, 15, 17, 21, 23, 24, 51, 54, 72, 88, 96, 117
Finland, ix, 47, 49, 64, 65, 79, 93, 97, 117

Index

firms, vii, 12, 17, 37, 45, 46, 47, 48, 49, 51, 54, 56, 58, 67, 68, 70, 71, 72, 75, 76, 77, 88, 99, 100, 105, 110, 111, 116
fiscal policy, 18, 80, 82, 87
fisheries, 73
flexibility, 16, 18, 19, 20, 24, 32, 50, 82
fluorescent lamps, 24
focusing, 78
food, 31, 32
food aid, 31
foreign banks, 108
foreign exchange, 54, 75, 87, 117
foreign exchange market, 54
foreign investment, 87
France, 40, 41, 45, 47, 52, 58, 61, 64, 65, 67, 79, 82, 83, 111, 115, 117
Freddie Mac, 49, 110
free trade, 30
free trade agreement, 30
freedom, 43, 72, 75
friction, 69
FSA, 96, 97, 98
FSAP, 76
funding, 14, 20, 27, 47, 51, 54, 59, 62, 90, 96, 99, 105
funds, 13, 20, 24, 27, 36, 40, 42, 46, 52, 54, 56, 58, 62, 67, 71, 76, 81, 82, 91, 96, 97, 100, 105, 107, 111, 118
furniture, 62

G

G-7, 55, 82
GDP, 14, 16, 18, 32, 44, 45, 60, 61, 63, 68, 71, 80, 83, 94, 96, 99, 105, 107, 108, 109, 115
GDP per capita, 109
Germany, 40, 41, 43, 45, 47, 55, 58, 59, 61, 64, 65, 66, 79, 82, 83, 111, 117
global demand, 55
global economy, 90
global markets, 30
global trade, 30, 36
GNP, 32
goals, 13, 18, 32, 40, 56, 57, 63, 71, 72, 80

goods and services, 94
Gordon Brown, 50, 97
governance, 15, 32, 33, 42, 58
government budget, 66, 68, 72, 80, 87
government securities, 81, 87
grants, 21, 27
Great Britain, 97
Greece, 43, 47, 55, 64, 65, 79, 117
Gross Domestic Product (GDP), 44, 94, 105, 108
groups, 21, 43, 96, 107
growth, vii, 11, 13, 14, 18, 19, 22, 24, 27, 29, 30, 31, 32, 36, 37, 38, 40, 44, 45, 46, 53, 54, 55, 56, 57, 60, 63, 66, 71, 72, 80, 86, 87, 88, 89, 90, 94, 95, 96, 99, 109, 112
guidance, 19, 74
guidelines, 22, 58, 59, 66, 79, 80, 108
guiding principles, 72

H

handling, 49, 68, 77
hands, 13, 57, 107
harbour, 33
harmonization, 76
health, vii, ix, 24, 86, 91, 107
health insurance, 107
hedge funds, 40, 46, 81, 118
hedging, 59
high tech, 63
high-level, 41, 74
high-speed, 24
hiring, 21, 23
HM Treasury, 80, 84
homeowners, 95
Hong Kong, 51
households, 12, 17, 19, 21, 24, 37, 64, 65, 67, 87
housing, 24, 46, 47, 61, 62, 68, 86, 87, 95, 110
human, 13, 63
human capital, 63
Hungary, 38, 39, 41, 64, 65, 79, 117
hybrid, 96

I

Iceland, v, vii, ix, 38, 48, 64, 65, 71, 81, 84, 93, 94, 95, 96, 97, 98, 99, 100, 101, 105, 112, 115, 117, 118
ICT, 22, 24, 27
illiquid asset, 113
imbalances, 17, 51, 99
implementation, viii, 17, 20, 21, 24, 27, 33, 48, 57, 78, 85, 114
import prices, 68
imports, 72, 94, 97, 99
incentive, 61
incentives, 18, 21, 24, 27, 91
inclusion, 21, 58
income, 17, 18, 60, 61, 67, 68, 96, 98, 108, 111, 113
income tax, 60, 61, 68, 98, 111
incomes, 21
independence, 73, 89, 90
India, 31
industrialized countries, 108
industry, vii, 11, 24, 27, 51, 52, 58, 62, 67
inflation, 19, 44, 72, 80, 87, 88, 94, 95, 99, 107
inflationary pressures, 55, 95, 97
infrastructure, 18, 20, 24, 27, 42, 60, 61, 62, 63, 65, 67, 112
initial public offerings, 89
injection, 50, 53, 82, 112
injections, 47, 48
innovation, 12, 13, 20, 22, 23, 27, 57
instability, 15, 37
institutions, viii, ix, 35, 36, 39, 45, 50, 51, 54, 69, 70, 71, 73, 78, 85, 86, 87, 89, 91, 96, 100, 103, 106, 110, 111, 114, 116
instruments, 17, 24, 31, 76, 86, 99
insurance, 47, 48, 50, 51, 76, 81, 86, 96, 99, 107, 118
insurance companies, 86
integration, viii, 21, 27, 36, 43, 70, 71, 73, 76, 80, 100
intellectual property, 31
Intelligence Community, 79
interbank market, 47, 54, 96, 99
interdependence, 39, 69, 105
interest rates, 15, 46, 48, 51, 53, 55, 60, 63, 72, 74, 86, 87, 88, 94, 95, 105, 107, 110, 112
international financial institutions, 32, 40, 117
international markets, ix, 39, 69, 103, 116
International Monetary Fund (IMF), ix, 38, 39, 40, 41, 44, 45, 46, 48, 50, 53, 55, 58, 81, 91, 93, 94, 96, 97, 98, 101, 108, 110, 113, 117
international relations, 107
international trade, 53, 97
internet, 27
intervention, 54, 56, 111
investment, vii, 11, 12, 13, 15, 17, 20, 22, 24, 27, 30, 32, 46, 47, 51, 56, 57, 62, 63, 71, 75, 76, 77, 80, 86, 87, 95, 96, 100, 101, 107, 110
investment bank, 96
investors, 49, 71, 95, 96, 97, 100
Ireland, 43, 47, 55, 64, 65, 79, 115, 117
Israel, 62
Italy, 40, 41, 45, 47, 58, 62, 64, 65, 79, 82, 111, 117

J

Japan, 31, 45, 82, 110, 117
job creation, 22
job training, 63
jobs, 13, 14, 19, 24, 31, 32, 56, 57, 60, 62, 66
jurisdictions, 37, 44, 54, 116

K

knowledge economy, 13
Korea, 82, 117

L

labor, 13, 18, 20, 21, 57, 67, 82
labor force, 67

Index

labor market, 13, 20, 21
lack of confidence, 56, 110, 111
Lamfalussy, 78, 79, 80
large banks, 70, 81
large-scale, 46, 65, 66
Latvia, 38, 41, 79, 117
laundering, 76, 117
law, 71, 76, 78, 100, 114
laws, 43, 72, 75, 76, 79, 84, 89, 97, 105, 106, 118
layoffs, 105
leadership, 52
legislation, 73, 75, 76, 78, 79, 80, 97
lender of last resort, ix, 50, 93, 99, 115
lenders, 48
lending, 15, 16, 22, 23, 32, 56, 59, 67, 81, 86, 87, 99, 107, 110
liberalization, 86, 95
likelihood, 37, 77
liquid assets, 113
liquidate, viii, 85
liquidation, 113
liquidity, 15, 23, 45, 46, 47, 48, 49, 50, 51, 53, 55, 56, 59, 72, 74, 86, 89, 99, 110, 111, 112, 113
Lisbon Strategy, 12, 13, 14, 16, 19, 20, 56, 63, 72, 80
Lithuania, 41, 79, 117
loans, 15, 22, 23, 27, 30, 33, 38, 43, 51, 52, 54, 58, 61, 62, 66, 68, 86, 87, 88, 89, 90, 91, 95, 97, 99, 105, 112, 113
local authorities, 27
London, 40, 51, 81
losses, viii, 58, 60, 70, 81, 85, 90, 91, 100, 115, 118
lower prices, 30
low-income, 67
Luxembourg, 40, 47, 50, 64, 65, 79, 117

M

Maastricht Treaty, 80, 82
machinery, 24
machines, 24, 27

macroeconomic, 42, 58, 60, 63, 66, 72, 80, 86, 107, 111
macroeconomic policies, 58, 72, 80
Malta, 79, 117
management, 57, 59, 67, 77, 89, 100, 107, 114
mandates, 79
manufacturing, 27
market discipline, viii, 78, 85, 90
market prices, 88
market segment, 69, 116
market value, 43, 98
marketplace, ix, 103, 104
measures, vii, ix, 15, 17, 19, 21, 24, 27, 32, 33, 36, 42, 43, 50, 52, 57, 58, 60, 63, 64, 65, 66, 67, 68, 69, 72, 75, 76, 79, 80, 86, 95, 97, 111, 112, 113, 114
Mediterranean, 30
membership, 40, 75
mergers, 43, 49, 75
Mexico, 82, 117
military, 62
Millennium, 31
Millennium Development Goals, 31
modalities, 30
models, 24, 42
Moldova, 38
monetary expansion, 72
monetary policy, x, 15, 36, 38, 40, 48, 50, 53, 60, 72, 81, 87, 95, 104, 107, 116
monetary union, 73
money, 24, 43, 46, 49, 51, 60, 62, 67, 68, 76, 81, 87, 96, 99, 107, 117
money laundering, 76, 117
money markets, 49, 51, 96, 99
money supply, 60
monopoly, 40, 48, 116
moratorium, 98
mortgage, 46, 47, 49, 51, 56, 81, 86, 87, 90, 95, 108, 109, 110, 113, 118
mortgage securitization, 46
mortgage-backed securities, 46
mortgages, 46, 90, 95, 108, 113
motion, 50, 98
movement, 59, 73

N

multilateral, 44, 58
mutual funds, 76

nation, 42, 58, 67, 70, 86, 97, 99
national action, 12
national debt, 80, 83
national economies, vii, ix, 39, 69, 71, 100, 103, 116
national policy, 86
Netherlands, 40, 41, 47, 58, 59, 62, 64, 65, 79, 111, 115, 117
network, 27, 30
New York, 82, 83, 91, 101
New York Times, 83, 91, 101
New Zealand, 82, 117
non-binding, 79, 80
Norway, ix, 47, 49, 53, 58, 63, 64, 65, 82, 93, 97, 111, 117

O

obligations, 51, 81, 97
OECD, 63, 65, 83, 94, 108, 117
oil, 44
online, 84, 97
open economy, 105
open market operations, 50
open markets, 30
opposition, 68
Organization for Economic Cooperation and Development, 39, 65, 83, 94, 108, 117
oversight, vii, ix, 39, 41, 42, 52, 69, 70, 79, 103, 104, 116
ownership, 52, 88, 113

P

pan-European, 24
Paris, 67
Parkinson, 82
Parliament, 24, 32, 67, 97, 106
participatory democracy, 79
partnerships, 24, 27
pension, 76, 96, 107
per capita, 108, 109
per capita income, 108
planned investment, 24, 27
play, ix, 15, 16, 31, 32, 39, 66, 69, 104, 107, 116
Poland, 38, 41, 54, 64, 65, 79, 82, 117
policy initiative, 74
policy instruments, 57
policy levels, vii
policy responses, viii, 35, 37, 44, 109
policymakers, 38, 39, 45, 104, 116
political instability, viii, 35, 38
political stability, 70
portfolio, 108, 113
portfolio management, 108
portfolios, 75
ports, 61
Portugal, 47, 58, 62, 64, 65, 79, 111, 117
postponement, 61, 68
power, 18, 19, 21, 24
powers, 40, 97
premium, 18
premiums, 81, 118
president, 80, 83
President Bush, 60, 111
pressure, vii, 11, 24, 32, 37, 48, 68, 95, 116
price stability, 107
prices, vii, 11, 19, 44, 46, 68, 77, 87, 88, 95, 109, 113
prisons, 61
private, vii, viii, 11, 15, 22, 23, 24, 27, 36, 41, 56, 57, 80, 87, 88, 89, 90, 99, 107
private banks, 108
private firms, viii, 36
private investment, 56, 80
private sector, 22, 24, 27, 57, 87, 88, 90
producers, 27
productivity, 20, 27, 57
program, ix, 48, 59, 62, 66, 81, 93, 96
property, iv, 24, 31, 47, 87, 88
prosperity, 20
protection, 21, 23, 33, 75, 77, 105, 113, 114
protectionism, 40

Index

public employment, 21
public finance, 16, 19
public funds, 27, 91
public housing, 61, 68
public investment, 17, 24, 67
public policy, 18
public resources, 37
public sector, 87
purchasing power, 18, 19, 21

R

R&D, 22, 24, 27, 57, 62
R&D investments, 27
rail, 61
range, 22, 27, 50, 51, 57, 67, 75, 80, 87, 99, 106, 107, 110, 117
ratings, 46
real estate, 46, 86, 87, 88, 90, 95, 113
rebates, 60, 111
recession, viii, 12, 13, 14, 18, 35, 37, 38, 44, 60, 66, 70, 71, 72, 111, 112
recognition, 75, 76
reconstruction, 15
recovery, 15, 17, 18, 19, 30, 33, 37, 42, 56, 69, 72, 90, 108
recovery plan, 19
reforms, vii, 14, 19, 20, 38, 44, 57, 58, 70, 87, 114
regulation, ix, 39, 40, 41, 42, 57, 69, 70, 72, 75, 76, 77, 103, 116
regulations, 40, 44, 52, 55, 75, 76, 79, 80, 84, 89, 114, 118
regulators, 69, 71, 78, 79, 80, 84, 100, 116, 118
regulatory capital, 88
regulatory framework, 36
research and development, 62
Reserve Bank of New Zealand, 82
reserve currency, 53
reserves, 16, 50, 54, 87, 117
resilience, 19
resolution, viii, 85, 89, 90, 97, 98, 104
resources, 16, 17, 27, 36, 37, 38, 40, 56, 70, 71, 78, 94, 100, 105

restructuring, 52, 63, 106
retail, 43, 47, 76, 77, 90
retail deposit, 47
retained earnings, 58
retaliation, 72
retention, 18
returns, 13
reunification, 87, 88
revenue, 17
risk, 12, 15, 18, 24, 33, 38, 42, 46, 52, 53, 57, 58, 68, 77, 86, 87, 90, 91, 96
risk management, 57, 58, 78
risks, vii, 11, 15, 42, 58, 78, 81, 84, 99, 113, 114, 115, 118
roadmap, 40
Romania, 38, 41, 79, 117
rural, 24, 108
rural areas, 108
rural development, 24
Russia, 31

S

safety, 27, 37, 111
savings, 23, 24, 66, 76, 96, 108
savings banks, 96, 108
savings rate, 66
Scandinavia, 96
school, 62, 65
search, viii, 35, 36, 37, 38
secretariat, 117
securities, 46, 47, 49, 51, 54, 56, 59, 71, 75, 76, 79, 81, 96, 98, 100, 107, 118
Securities and Exchange Commission, 107
security, viii, 13, 24, 31, 32, 35, 37, 57, 81, 82
self-employment, 21
Senate, 79
September 11, 91
Serbia, 38
services, iv, 20, 21, 23, 24, 27, 37, 43, 46, 73, 75, 76, 77, 79, 80, 94, 107, 110, 117
SGP, 80, 82
Shanghai, 51
shareholders, 47, 67

shares, 40, 50, 52, 53, 55, 59, 77, 97
sharing, 14, 15, 106
short period, vii, 36
short run, viii, 19, 35, 38
shortage, 54
short-term, 17, 18, 19, 20, 24, 30, 50, 53, 54, 56, 57, 81, 87, 95, 96, 99, 107, 110, 117
short-term interest rate, 95
short-term liabilities, 107
Singapore, 82
single currency, 43
single market, 12, 14
Slovakia, 41, 79, 117
Slovenia, 79, 117
Small Business Act, 22, 23
smart com, 20
SME, 23
SMEs, 18, 22, 23, 27, 33
social benefits, 61, 63
social housing, 24
solidarity, 37
solvency, ix, 45, 56, 93, 99, 111
Spain, 40, 45, 47, 58, 62, 64, 65, 79, 111, 115, 117
spectrum, 27
speed, 20, 23, 24, 27, 29, 77
spillovers, 29
stability, viii, 12, 15, 18, 19, 35, 37, 38, 42, 69, 70, 71, 74, 107
Stability and Growth Pact, 12, 14, 16, 18, 32, 43, 57, 63, 66, 80, 82
stabilization, ix, 48, 93, 96
stabilize, 36, 38, 48, 72, 97, 111, 112
stabilizers, 66
stages, 50, 51
stakeholder, 89
stakeholders, 27
standards, 24, 33, 42, 46, 57, 58, 78, 79, 80, 114
state aid, 22, 23, 67
state-owned, 63
stimulus, 16, 17, 19, 20, 36, 38, 42, 43, 44, 57, 60, 61, 62, 63, 65, 66, 67, 68, 69, 71, 72, 91, 95, 111, 112

stock, vii, 11, 24, 51, 58, 75, 76, 82, 87, 88, 89, 107, 115
stock exchange, 75, 89, 107
stock markets, vii, 11
strategic management, 107
strategies, 18, 21, 59
strength, 99
stress, 51, 56, 58, 115
structural funds, 24
structural reforms, 13, 14, 16, 17, 19, 57
sub-prime, 46, 109
subsidies, 18, 21, 23, 27, 66
supervision, ix, 39, 41, 42, 44, 52, 57, 69, 70, 72, 76, 86, 93, 100, 103, 107, 116
supervisors, 42, 58, 59, 73, 78
suppliers, 27, 67
surveillance, 73
sustainability, 13, 17, 18, 19
sustainable development, 32
sustainable growth, 24, 31, 32
Sweden, v, vii, viii, ix, 41, 47, 49, 53, 55, 59, 63, 64, 65, 79, 82, 85, 86, 87, 88, 89, 90, 91, 93, 97, 105, 110, 112, 117, 118
Switzerland, v, vii, ix, 47, 53, 59, 63, 64, 65, 103, 104, 105, 106, 107, 108, 109, 110, 112, 113, 115, 117, 118
systemic risk, 41, 114

T

takeover, 49, 97, 110
targets, 24, 27, 32
tariffs, 30
tax cuts, 17, 61, 66, 67
tax deduction, 62
tax increase, 17, 61, 68
tax system, 87
taxation, 16, 18
taxes, 18, 27, 60, 61, 62, 68, 95, 111
taxpayers, 87, 89
telecommunications, 42, 60, 61, 63
terminals, 75
terrorism, 71, 97, 100
terrorist, 117
theft, 81, 118

Index

thermal energy, 94
threat, 44
threatened, viii, 85, 99
threatening, 59
threshold, 33
time consuming, 78
time frame, 18
top management, 67
trade, 29, 30, 36, 40, 53, 58, 72, 73, 77, 95, 97, 99
trade deficit, 95, 99
trading, 61, 62, 75, 76, 97, 107
traffic, 27
training, 21, 23, 63, 80
transactions, 39, 53, 75, 76, 89
transfer, 98, 113
transformation, 50, 110
transition, 27
transitions, 20, 57
transparency, 40, 56, 58, 70, 77, 90
transparent, viii, 85
transport, 22, 23, 24
Treasury, 49, 53, 56, 80, 81, 82, 84, 97, 101, 107, 110, 111
Treasury bills, 81
Treasury Department, 56
treaties, 73
trust, 99
turbulence, 15, 50
Turkey, 64, 65, 117

U

U.S. Department of the Treasury, 82, 107
U.S. economy, 60, 90, 111
U.S. Treasury, 49, 53, 56, 82, 110
UK, vii, 50, 52, 68, 81, 83, 84, 101
Ukraine, 38, 41
uncertainty, 55
unemployment, vii, 11, 12, 13, 17, 21, 37, 57, 58, 62, 66, 87, 88
unemployment rate, 88
UNFCCC, 31
uninsured, 91

United Kingdom, 40, 45, 47, 52, 53, 59, 61, 64, 65, 67, 79, 82, 96, 105, 115, 117
United Nations, 108
United States, viii, ix, 35, 36, 37, 38, 39, 40, 43, 44, 45, 46, 47, 48, 49, 53, 54, 56, 69, 70, 71, 72, 82, 85, 89, 90, 96, 100, 103, 104, 107, 116, 117
universities, 21, 61
university students, 86

V

vacancies, 21
value added tax, 61, 62, 68
values, 46, 47, 78, 86, 89, 90, 95
VAT, 18, 21, 24, 68
vehicles, 24, 27, 47
voting, 97
vulnerability, 99

W

wages, 66
Wall Street Journal, 80, 81, 82, 83, 84
Washington Post, 79, 80, 83
weakness, 41
wealth, 37
Western Europe, 38, 41
wholesale, 47, 54, 76
workers, 13, 21, 22, 58, 61, 62, 63, 68, 82, 83
World Bank, 38, 80
World Economic Forum, ix, 103, 104
World Trade Organization, 108
WTO, 30, 108

Y

yield, 39

Z

zero growth, vii, 11